tellwell

Tellwell Talent
www.tellwell.ca

ISBN
978-1-77370-799-0 (Hardcover)
978-1-77370-800-3 (Paperback)
978-1-77370-801-0 (eBook)

TABLE OF CONTENTS

Why did I write this book? I wrote this book for you. Simple as that. I want you to be able to *live* your life how you *really* want to. So many people are stuck living as a reaction to the problems they experience throughout their lives—some of which occurred in the past, some of which occur daily.

So many people are saddled with negative beliefs of their worth, or their abilities; and so many individuals are stuck repeating the same old patterns of their personal life's drama. Many people believe these patterns are simply "the way it is" for them, not realizing that their destiny isn't about suffering or managing their way through their suffering—because it's not! It's about something different. Your destiny is about what happens *after you get through that suffering.* But, you must *want* to get through it, otherwise, you will be destined to repeat that suffering over, and over, and over again.

This book will help you awaken yourself to the reality of your suffering (where it comes from and why), and then show you how easy it can be to get relief. Spoiler-alert: I recommend that you *seriously* consider a type of therapy called, Eye Movement Desensitization and Reprocessing (EMDR), as your vehicle to take you to your destination of relief. That's right: EMDR. Nothing else comes close.

If you want *real* results that let you know your life is *actually changing*, and you want these results in considerably less time than you would probably get with "regular talk therapy," then EMDR is for you. If you're looking to "hang out" with your counsellor and have a conversation that you could have with a close friend over a coffee...then EMDR is probably not for you—at least not yet. EMDR cuts right through the surface fluff and gets to the heart of your pain, that is, the memories responsible for them.

Let me tell you a little bit about suffering. There's all kinds of it out there, and I want you to know that I'm no stranger to it. Before I began my career as psychotherapist, and well before I started my education in psychology, *my suffering was my education.* I learned what emotional pain felt like, and I found out early in my life, that this was a feeling that I wouldn't wish on anybody. Let me share with you a little bit about my story. I think it's important that we get to know each other—that's how we build trust.

Picture this scene: It's dusk now. The sun is setting over the horizon of this beautiful resort in the Caribbean, overlooking a white, sandy beach. The waves of the Atlantic Ocean brush onto the shore like the eyelids of Mother Nature as she looks back at me. The warm, yet salty breeze gently sways the palm trees back and forth, as they make a light rustle. I feel like I'm cocooned on the 12th floor balcony, as I'm sipping on a rum and coke in a little plastic hotel-room cup. My partner is next to me—a beautiful young woman for whom I've fallen deeply in love with. Her black hair frames her athletic face, and her eyes tell stories of her depth that I fear I can never know. I believe I will marry this soul one day.

She looks over to me, and says, "You're a worthless, filthy piece of shit. You and your diseased cock will always be alone, and no one will ever love you...except maybe your prostitutes."

My heart sinks into the bottom of my stomach. The shame I feel touches my essence, and suddenly I'm feeling rage as defiance begins to bubble through my veins. I look at her in shock, as I begin to process what she's just said to me. I start to defend myself, and lash out at her, calling her names like "gold digger," "slut," and whatever else I could use to protect myself. Suddenly I become aware of the amount of expense that I've incurred to bring this woman to tropical paradise, and how little I feel I'm being appreci-ated. For a struggling student working in the ghettos of Vancouver,

British Columbia (that's the Downtown Eastside for those of you unfamiliar), CAD $5,000+ is a lot of money. At this point, I'm aware of how awful this relationship truly is, and how "broken" we really are. I begin to feel the grief as I allow the relationship to settle into reality, away from the fantasy of perfection, where it was just a few minutes ago.

I get up to leave and she begins to hit me. She slaps my face and punches me in the chest. (I don't remember where else she hit me, or how many times, but I remember trying to close the balcony door and lock her outside.) She keeps her leg braced in between the sliding door and the wall. At this point we are screaming at each other. It's a kind of anger and hostility that I've never seen before. Finally, I give up. Fine. There's no use fighting. She slams the door open and storms to the other end of the hotel room. I'm looking at her from just in front of the balcony now. She turns around, glaring at me. I've never seen anyone look at me so. And in a flash of a moment, she's sprinting to the edge of the balcony...and she jumps. My stomach drops...

...

...

...

Let's rewind about a decade and a half earlier:

I'm 11-years old. I'm staring deeply into my full-length mirror, at those big, brown eyes that meet me in return. They seem to see into my very soul. My eyelids begin burning as a single tear begins running down my face. I feel heat rising from under my cheeks; it's spreading now like wildfire through my throat, shoulders, and chest as I flex my flabby arms. It starts off as a silent protest, with just a sense...nothing more. Then, suddenly, I *scream* to myself as if the Heavens can hear me without words, "You're fat! You're disgusting! You're a piece of shit. Nobody likes you. **This** is why you're alone. You're ugly."

These words hurt so much, I can barely stand it. I begin beating myself. *THUMP!* As I punch my gut. *SMACK!* As I slap my breasts thinking, "Men aren't supposed to *have* breasts." I can feel the blood vessels burst as I pinch my fat under my arms, leaving bruises, and I can see the hand marks I leave as I try to peel my stomach off my body. *Ahh*, I breathe a sigh of relief.

I was inflicting physical pain on myself so that I could distract myself away from the emotional pain I experienced deep inside.

It was not until later in my life that I recognized my anger with God, and life itself, was due to my unhappiness with *my* life. Why was I leading this life? Why was I "the fat kid" who was always alone? Why couldn't I have been born into the athlete's life who got all the girls and had tons of male friends, and got to strut around with the masculine, testosterone-fuelled body? Why was I always just so alone? Why did I have to feel like I was always looking in from outside my life's window, at all those people who seemed so happy to have their relationships and fun? These sorts of questions would deepen my anger and self-loathing, because as I became aware of what I was not, I became aware of what I was. And I didn't like me. No...in fact *I hated me.*

It was still early in my life when I decided to be a "good boy" and to be of service to others. I thought that if I could be of service to others that would mean that they wouldn't hate me, and if I they wouldn't hate me, then I must have *some* value.

First, I became a reiki and a massage practitioner. I'd always be the "guy that others would come and talk to about their problems." Later, I began working in the Downtown Eastside as an outreach worker—helping homeless men access services that would eventually help them to reintegrate themselves back into society. I thought to myself, "This is what good people do." Honestly, it *did* feel good to help people, and I even had some wonderful co-workers who I would hang out with on the weekends. I had friends, but I felt alone.

I would often sit by myself in some bar drinking and thinking about my life, and about how shitty I *really* was. My life kept repeating the same patterns over and over and over, getting more and more entrenched. It left me feeling ashamed.

Then I met her: I met the girl I would later take to that Caribbean paradise, in a dingy bar in my hometown. I fell in love almost instantly. She was fun, exotic, and had just enough problems in her life that I felt that I would be important to her too—I thought I could "fix" her.

Some nights we would fight for what seemed like eternity. She would scream at me calling me names like "stupid" and "worthless," and she'd threaten to "knock my big nose off my face." When she would say these things to me, it reminded me of the girl I lost my virginity to (she was abusive as well). Then, we would apologize to each other and make-up. We'd tell each other that we loved each other, and that we hadn't really meant what we had said. The honeymoon phase of the make-up would be amazing. We'd feel even more connected to each other because we just shared the bond of conflict and resolution. We saw each other at our worst, and then accepted each other afterwards. Then we went on vacation, and we had the fight that would prove to be our last fight...

She bolts towards me from the other side of the room, tears staining her flushed face, and jumps towards me and the balcony railing. Instinctively, I grab her with my right arm. Holding her tight, I drag her away from the railing, back into the room (with what seemed like superhuman strength), and pin her to the bed. I hold her, as she thrashes about, clawing her nails into my arms and neck. I have her pinned sideways like I'm holding down a wild animal. She's screaming, and I'm screaming back. I tell her to stop, that we are done. She's about to go home, alone, on a plane tomorrow morning.

Finally, hotel security enters the room and divides us up, placing me in another room on a different floor. I am so shaken up I don't know what to do but to drink.

I keep drinking.

The next day I am at the pool bar, drunk and crying. I feel betrayed by life. I met this perfect person and she turns out to be a terrifying monster? I would forever be alone. If *she* didn't accept me and my flaws, then *nobody* would. The words, "I am worthless," keep repeating in my head. After countless double rum and cokes (many of them free from the hotel bartenders and some concerned guests), I realize: I've been repeating the same patterns over and over again. And until I heal the underlying reasons for these patterns, I am destined to keep repeating them.

So, that's what I did: I healed.

Why do I tell you all of this about myself? Because you, like me, have underlying patterns of negativity that keep repeating. Until you decide to *really* heal them, they will *not* go away. Believe me. Until you—just now—only a handful of people knew these parts of my life's trauma story. If you had caught me at any time throughout my past, you wouldn't have known any of it. I kept all of it packed down below the surface. I denied the existence of my shadow impulses for most of my life—and then they'd come out in ingloriously disastrous ways. My issues didn't go away because I tried to stop thinking about them. You know the saying, "Out of sight, out of mind?" Yeah, it's bullshit. My issues festered, grew, and infected every area of my life. The feelings of worthlessness bled into my work with clients, it bled into my relationships, it bled into the belief that my dreams were unattainable.

I want you to stop your bleeding. If you truly want to change, you NEED therapy. Specifically, you need EMDR therapy. The information you will receive inside this book will change your life's direction. When you use EMDR to neutralize your traumatic memories, and to put an end to the destructive life patterns that you keep repeating, you will thank yourself—I guarantee it. I have.

Now, *I know that I am valuable*, with or without my advanced training in EMDR and my professional degrees. *I matter regardless* of how many people I help with my skills. *I am important* to my new partner because I spend the time to let her matter to me, not because I think either of us need "fixing." I *know* that my purpose in life is to help alleviate the suffering of others in our world—not to get drunk on the weekends, or to plan the next vacation. I sleep to gather energy to grow and to help others transform.

Your transcendence out of your suffering is what my business is built upon. I *want* to become a beacon for you to know that you can change your life too, if you *really want to*. You don't *need* to go through your life worrying about how you are being perceived by others. You don't *need* to feel "less-than." You don't *need* to keep repeating your negative patterns of dysfunction.

You *deserve* to feel important, worthwhile, and valuable. You *deserve* to have love, be loved, and live your life with passion. You *deserve* to regret nothing.

You *deserve* to be free.

I dedicate this book to my clients, both past and new. Thank you for *you*, for your courage has taught me more than you could ever know.

WHY DO YOU **NEED** THIS BOOK?

Good question. Before we go into why you *need* this book, let me ask you a few questions. And before you think to yourself, "Oh great, he's going to ask me to reflect on some psychobabble mumbo-jumbo…," I want to make you a promise: Reading this book will be worth it. If you are unsure as to what EMDR (Eye Movement Desensitization and Reprocessing) is, or whether it's right for you, you *need* to read this. Even if you've never even *heard* of EMDR before, but you are aware that you are tired of suffering in your life, you *need* to read this. I promise you, it will be worth it.

Here come those questions (brace yourself, there's a few of them).

First, are you completely satisfied with your life as a "whole"? Take a second to think about it…probably not, right? So, let's get a bit more specific. Are you completely satisfied with your love life? Are you able to be completely intimate (emotionally and sexually) with your partner (or yourself)? Do you go from relationship to relationship, or from partner to partner, without ever fully committing to anyone? Do you keep getting your heart broken?

If you're married or in a relationship, are you quick to fight with your partner, or do you prefer to stay quiet—afraid of conflict and the repercussions? Are you afraid to let those close to you, really "see" you?

Are you able to accept yourself as you are—body, mind, *and* spirit? Do you *love* your body? Do you *love* yourself (your good, your bad, and your "ugly")?

How's your career going? If you have one, are you completely fulfilled by it? Or is it simply a means to an end—i.e. it pays for you to "live your life on the weekends"? Why is that?

If you don't have a career, why not? Do you make enough money? Do you have more than enough to provide for yourself, your family, and for your creative endeavours? Money is a basic necessity these days, so, do you have enough? Or do you struggle? Have you been living paycheck-to-paycheck, never getting afloat, just treading water above a sea of debt? Or worse, are you slowly sinking further and further into the red? Do you know how to invest your money and make your *money* make **more money**? If you don't, do you know how to find the right people to help you figure that out?

Do you suffer from bouts of depression? Is it hard to get out of bed in the mornings, or to go to sleep at night? Do you eat too much or too little? Have you thought of suicide before? (I have.) Have you tried hurting yourself? Cutting, burning, hitting, etc.? Or how about less obvious ways of hurting yourself, like drinking, drug abuse, or another kind of self-sabotage?

If you were to be diagnosed with a terminal illness and you only had the rest of today to live, would you say that your life was meaningful? Do you have any regrets? Who would be there with you as you died? What would people say about you during your funeral? Would you have left anything behind for others—money, fame, or an important social cause?

OK. So, I asked you a lot more than a few questions. Take a deep breath. My goal was not to completely depress you with your answers, but only to jump right into the reality of your life at this very moment and help to paint the picture as to why you really *need* this book.

If your answers were less than ideal (and I mean you weren't fudging them at all), then you've got a little bit of work to do to correct your life's course. And, trust me on this one: After you learn what I'm going to teach you with this book, you'll discover that correcting your life's course is going to be easier than you ever thought—and faster.

I'm going to make a bold statement here, so pardon the capitals: **EVERY NEGATIVE ANSWER you gave is due to one or more negative core beliefs about yourself that you gathered because of negative and/or traumatic experiences that occurred earlier in your life.** These negative core beliefs coming from these past experiences exist in "real-time" because the original experience(s) were **NOT PROPERLY processed** and remain as "raw data" in different neuro-networks in your brain. Seriously, all your negative symptoms and negative life patterns occur because your brain is currently "wired" to seek out, or to somehow find yourself in situations or with people, who "confirm" your negative core beliefs—this, in turn, allows you to keep your negative core beliefs and further perpetuate those negative patterns.

What do I mean by "negative core beliefs"? I'm glad you asked. A negative core belief is a statement that you say to yourself, and for which *feels real*. Sometimes people experience this literally as "words" that they repeat in their mind to themselves, and for others, they literally *feel* it, in their body—either way this is something that runs *deep inside to the core of your current identity*. When we touch on a negative core belief, we know it is there because we not only know it cognitively, but we experience corresponding emotions that are localized inside the body. Most times, these feelings are so powerful and so uncomfortable that we avoid them, because facing it feels like torture—like how paying taxes to the government feels, or nails on a chalkboard, or purposely sitting in front of a screaming child on public transit (actually, I'm just kidding, it's actually much worse). Our negative core beliefs are painful, and not many individuals move towards pain.

People do all sorts of things to avoid these feelings, like: drowning them in food, alcohol, or drugs; keeping oneself continuously occupied with work, sex, activities, other people's lives (our children's, friends', celebrities', etc.); and, sometimes, we even completely disconnect from our realities. The disconnection can be as harmless as binge-watching a few favourite shows (can anybody say, "Game of Thrones®?"); but it can be much worse such as <u>repression</u>, <u>dissociation</u>, or <u>denial</u>. We'll get to repression, and dissociation later, but if you are in denial about your own reality, then you remain powerless to change it. Ironically, the responsibility to change your life is yours, and yours alone. If you remain in denial, don't expect anyone to come and save you, because you won't be able to recognize their efforts anyway!

Many people, when faced with the opportunity to face the facts of their existence, utilize denial or deflection as a defense mechanism. They usually say something like, "Oh, you think *my* childhood was bad? What about all those children who are molested by their family members? Or what about those who grow up in poor countries without access to running water, food, or shelter? *That's bad.*" My answer to these statements is always: "Yes. Those childhood scenarios *are bad.*" There's no question that those early life experiences are going to leave a deep mark on one's psyche. But, there is also no question that other less obvious forms of childhood distress, leave their marks as well.

In the EMDR community, there is a difference between what we call, large-'T' traumas, and small-'t' traumas. Large-T traumas consist of the obvious sorts of traumas, such as: violence, rape, assaults, childhood abuse, surviving horrific accidents, or terrorist attacks, etc. Small-t traumas consist of the more ubiquitous forms of trauma, such as: schoolyard bullying, neglectful parenting, being rejected by peers or potential lovers, failing subjects in school, shaming, etc. The lists of these scenarios can go on and on, of course.

The effects of both forms of trauma are far-reaching and devastating. Nobody is helped by comparing their suffering to the suffering of others, so let's not do it. I believe we need to acknowledge that trauma is everywhere, and I think we've all sustained our fair share.

You don't have to believe me, but I think you should hear it from the "horse's mouth." Yes, I am calling myself a horse.

Our core beliefs are so powerful that they literally run our life's show—and you may not even be aware of it happening. Let me give you a personal example of how core beliefs can influence one's life (this one's a negative core belief).

I was bullied in school growing up. I was overweight and kind of a loner, even though I had many "friends." I wasn't particularly gifted academically, but I was rather artistically creative. I came from a family where my father was the only doctor in town for many years. We weren't *rich,* but I was provided with an upper-middle class childhood. I was really spoiled when it came to material possessions, however, I felt that I didn't matter. I didn't always repeat those words in my head, but rather, I felt this feeling in my solar plexus, and gut. No matter how many opportunities came where I got a good grade or was treated to a *sweet* family vacation (usually in the Caribbean), I felt <u>worthless</u> (before I even knew what that word *meant*).

I wished that I could have been born into the life of a sports jock—all those kids got the girls' attention easily, and they had such close friendships with others. I always struck out with my love life. I was good at making friends out of the girls I was attracted to, but not so much luck in the romance department. I felt like there was something *wrong with me.* I always attributed being rejected by the opposite sex as being due to my body—if I wasn't fat, they would like me. I also attributed being rejected by the boys for sports, or for extra-curricular activities, as being due to me being fat. The boys would bully me, calling me names like, "Short, Fat, With Glasses." My fatness was *proof* that I wasn't good enough—proof that I was worthless.

My go-to response for uncomfortable feelings was to push them way down deep inside somewhere and try and forget them (this is called repression). Essentially, I went on a mission to prove to myself that I was good enough. When I got in shape in university, I met and dated lots of women, had many sexual experiences, and hosted amazing parties in my dorm, and—no matter how much love and respect I got from my friends—I still *felt* worthless. My body was in shape, my grades were good (trending towards A+), I had friends, girlfriends, money—but still did not feel good enough. My core belief about myself was, "I'm not good enough." Every rejection from others, and even every negative facial or verbal twinge that I perceived as being about me, meant a *rejection*, and therefore meant that deep down, I didn't matter.

Hopefully you can see how my core belief that I was "not good enough" influenced how I went about my life. Due to this negative core belief, I was afraid of going out into the world because I felt I would be unable to succeed. I believed I would surely fail. After all, I assumed that when my first clients would get a whiff of my worthlessness, they wouldn't ever be able to fully *trust* that I could help them. I figured that they'd leave after the first session and never come back. What's commonly referred to as "imposter syndrome," for me, was all about me feeling worthless.

Since the belief started in my childhood, no matter how many accomplishments or good external experiences I had, the belief carried on inside of me—throughout my university years, and right through to the beginnings of my career as a psychotherapist. This experience is not unique to me. It's happened to you, too. You have at least one negative core belief inside of you that festers within your very core identity—polluting your ability to fully embrace your *true* inner potential. It might not be the belief "I'm not good enough," but trust me, you've got at least one in there.

So...why do you *NEED* this book? Because if you don't take the information in this book seriously, I'm afraid you will never change those negative core beliefs, and you will be destined to keep repeating the mediocre or destructive patterns that keep you stuck—living safe, living "small."

DON'T WORRY, YOU'RE NOT ALONE

If you want to make a change, you NEED therapy. And specifically, you need EMDR therapy. This is certainly a bold claim—and it's one where I hope that you can appreciate is made with the utmost honour and respect for you as an individual. Decades ago, psychotherapy was considered as being reserved only for "the crazy," "the weak," or for the truly rich...(*ahem*) women (as in the Freudian era); but the need for psychotherapeutic care has been growing so much that the warning signs are everywhere—you need only, to look at the facts.

Did you know that according to The Mental Health Commission of Canada (MHCC), one in five Canadians (6.7 million) experience a mental health problem or mental illness in any given year (2016)? To put that statistic into context, one in 25 (1.4 million) were diagnosed with heart disease, and one in 15 (2.2 million) were diagnosed with type 2 diabetes (MHCC, 2016). This means that you are far more likely to be diagnosed with a mental health condition, rather than heart disease or type 2 diabetes—and we all know how important screening for heart disease and diabetes are!

Did you know that the cost of mental health illness to the Canadian economy is more than $50 billion (CHCC, 2016)? **FIFTY BILLION!!**

And did you know that according to the Canadian Mental Health Association, each year, 5% of Canadians will be affected by an anxiety disorder (CMHA, 2018)? That may not seem like a high number right away, but when you consider that in 2016 (for example), the population in Canada was 36.29 million people—that meant that 1,814,500 people were experiencing an anxiety disorder that year. That's a lot of people! Furthermore, Statistics Canada suggests that at least 2.6% of Canadians aged 15 and older report symptoms consistent with Generalized Anxiety Disorder—that's nearly one *million* people (2013)!

Considering those who die of suicide, statistics show that 4,000 of these individuals were confronting a mental health problem or illness (MHCC, 2016). And what's worse? The MHCC suggests that only about one in three adults who were experiencing a mental health problem or illness ever bothered to seek out and receive services (2016). I wonder if this incredibly sparse number of individuals who received treatment is due to those not taking their mental health seriously, and therefore didn't look for help, or if the public health system is letting its people down by not providing affordable avenues for treatment. Either way, it's a number that is far too low for me.

What's quite troubling (if the numbers above aren't troubling enough!), is that only about one in five *children* ever get help for their mental health problems (CMHA, 2013), and we are all too aware that people whose issues develop during childhood tend to have more severe issues in their adulthood. Furthermore, 70% of those who were polled in Canadian prisons indicated that their mental health concerns began in childhood (MHCC, 2016).

I don't want to scare you and suggest that if you suffer from a mental health condition, you are somehow destined for the criminal justice system. No, the MHCC suggests just the opposite: Individuals who are suffering from a mental health concern are far more likely to be the *victims* of violence, rather than the perpetrators (2016).

Probably the most common mental health concern that individuals experience is "anxiety." The Anxiety Disorders Association of Canada (2007) has stated that at least 12% of Canadians will be diagnosed with an anxiety disorder in their lifetime—that's a staggeringly high number: 4,354,800! One in every 10 people will experience a panic attack in their lifetime (Tidy, 2016). And regarding our neighbours to the south, the Anxiety and Depression Association of America reported that 40 million American adults suffer from anxiety disorders, and only a third of the population undergo treatment (2016).

As you can tell, there are plenty of statistics to suggest that if you notice you are experiencing some difficulty with your mental health, you're not alone. In fact, I can easily make the statement that everyone suffers with some sort of mental health concern. It may not be a "diagnosable" problem, but I guarantee that everyone at some point in their life has struggled with something. These statistics only cover those who have reportedly sought mental health services. We'll cover some more statistics in just a moment, but I'd like to have a brief discussion about anxiety.

Anxiety is very normal and is something that everyone experiences. It is considered by many as providing a functional, evolutionary advantage, improving the human organism's chance for survival. The individual experiences anxiety related to survival situations as an elevated heart rate, pumping of adrenaline and other neurotransmitters, flushing in the face, and changes within the body's functions to slow down (and cease) digestion, and to promote blood flow to the extremities (arms and legs). Essentially, anxiety permits the individual to go from a state of "rest and digestion," to a state where they are ready to "fight" or to "flee" (there's two other responses as well, called "freeze" and "shut down," which I'll explain later).

Once the individual accesses the state of anxiety, they either avoid or conquer the threat, or they are conquered by the threat—that's it. Or that's how it was supposed to be in the early days of our human development, that is, when we lived together in small clans in the wild, where we hunted the legendary woolly mammoth and had to look out for sabre-toothed tigers.

If the individual survived the threat, the anxiety would immediately dissipate, and the body would return to a state of general rest, and then begin to digest food again. However, due to the fast-paced and highly-stressed lifestyles we live in today, the autonomic arousal (the body's natural response to increase anxiety to help one be ready to either fight, flee, or freeze in the face of potential danger) is often not permitted to reside, or to return to its natural baseline. When this occurs too frequently, the individual's body is affected in a greater capacity, such that the body is "fooled" into thinking that it is constantly in danger. In the past, the anxiety may have been because you were in danger of being a sabre-toothed tiger's dinner, but now, it might be that you experience anxiety because you worry that you will miss that deadline at work.

What makes matters worse is if the individual has experienced one or more consistent traumas in their life (such as early childhood abuse, bullying, parental neglect, etc.). When this happens, the baseline level of anxiety is often altered, so that the individual is consistently experiencing heightened arousal, and the body rarely experiences rest. When this persists for too long, the individual may develop one or more anxiety disorders (as well as a host of other potential illnesses).

"Anxiety disorders" differ from "normal anxiety" when anxiety tends to be more intense (as in panic attacks), last longer, and lead to phobias. Generally, those experiencing an anxiety disorder will experience great difficulty facing the root cause of the anxiety, or the worst-case scenario of the anxiety. Doing so typically causes people to feel like they're nearing an anxiety attack or panic attack. (For helpful resources on anxiety please visit my website at: www. GrigoreCounselling.com).

If you experience anxiety, you're not alone, and I encourage you to keep reading.

Let's turn our attention to depression, as it is another very common form of mental health distress.

When thinking about depression, we need to differentiate between two kinds, really. One, is the kind of low mood that happens after something bad happens to you in your life—your pet dies, you get fired, a family member becomes ill, or you simply had a really bad day (or two or three). It's certainly a common experience for people to have a low mood after some negative event just took place.

The second kind of depression we need to focus on is the kind of depression that doesn't go away after a couple days or a couple weeks. This sort of depression is becoming more serious. Naturally, there are particular disorders of depression that we could focus upon, but that won't be my focus here. You can easily Google® "depressive disorders" and you'll likely find much more detailed information. Of course, I encourage you to seek out a professional opinion if you are struggling with symptoms of depression.

Some common symptoms of depression are:

- experiencing consistently low mood
- becoming highly agitated or quick to become angry
- being constantly tired
- having trouble sleeping
- eating too much or too little
- feeling worthless
- feeling hopeless
- thinking about (and/or acting) on suicidal thoughts

If these symptoms do not go away after a few days or about a week, then it would be wise to check in with a mental health professional regarding your mood and to understand why you are feeling this way.

I believe that depression is very natural (in fact, you may notice that I believe almost every kind of mental health distress is "natural" because there's always a reason for experiencing what it is that we are experiencing). Based upon my earlier philosophical and practical experience with existentialist-informed psychology, I believe that depression is a *signal* from the deepest part of oneself—the Authentic Self (i.e. "the soul," or "unconscious") (Yalom, 1931, 1980). This signal is manifested by the Authentic Self as a message that, "There's something about how you're living your life that isn't quite alright." The more severe the depression, the stronger the signal from the Authentic Self.

Some believe that depression is solely an imbalance of neurotransmitters in the brain, which affect a person's mood, and sometimes I agree with that presentation of depression (depending on the person's situation, of course). Others will say depression is solely a result of one's environment. However, I believe we should not get caught up in the trap of a "chicken-or-egg" debate, as all factors in the individual's life are important—so it's likely a case of "chicken breast with a side of eggs."

How common is depression? *Common.* The World Health Organization, has stated that depression is one of the foremost causes of the worldwide disability and disease burden (Gauhar, 2016). According to the Canadian Mental Health Association, 8% of Canadians will experience major depression in their lifetime—that's just under three million people—and almost 400,000 people will develop bipolar disorder (2017)!

In my own practice and from my personal life experience, I have *not met one single person* (with whom I've had a serious conversation about depression with) that has not experienced at least one significant bout with depression. It is so common that I am willing to bet that you've not only experienced the symptoms of depression, and maybe that you, like me, have thought about suicide; maybe not to the degree that you've seriously considered taking your own life, but that the thought about "the end of you" has entered into your mind (suicide is a common thought as a way to relieve pain, to join loved ones, or to make up for some action that we feel guilt or remorse for). And if you've seriously thought about suicide, and/or have even tried to take your life—you're not alone. It's an unfortunate reality for many people.

Someone suffering from depression is at an increased risk for suicide (Bryan & Rudd, 2006). Simply thinking about it from time to time is quite a bit different than planning the method, time, and specifics of carrying out the action. Regardless, if you are having suicidal thoughts, this should be taken seriously, and some precautions should be created to ensure your safety (i.e. calling 9-1-1 or a crisis line, having support people close by, practicing some stress-management techniques, etc.).

Depression comes in all different manifestations. When I was depressed, I didn't find any joy in much of anything that I was doing. I didn't want to leave my apartment, and I just wanted to eat my way into oblivion. I would self-medicate with alcohol and drugs and engage in some risky sexual behaviour. And to top it all off, I spent A LOT of money in the process of trying to make myself feel better—both through therapy as well as via self-medication. If you took the time to have a deeper conversation with me, you might have discovered that I appeared sad about something. But if you *didn't* take the time to communicate deeply with me, you would never have known that I was depressed. I pulled off looking "normal" really, really well!

Now, even though sadness is the obvious indicator that someone may be suffering with depression, it is also common for *anger* to be an expression of depression. Almost anything can set off individuals who display their depression as anger. Others do not display their depression at all; they laugh and smile and appear "normal." In my humble opinion, these are the individuals in the most danger from depression—nobody can help them because they don't appear to need any help. (For more information on identifying depression, please see my website at: www.GrigoreCounselling.com.)

Now, if you didn't see yourself in descriptions of anxiety or depression above, you may be wondering, "What about *my* distress?" Great question, let's address that.

If you know that you are experiencing something a little bit more serious or unique, such as PTSD (Post-Traumatic Stress Disorder), OCD (Obsessive Compulsive Disorder), an eating disorder, a phobia, or something that you can't quite describe but you know that *something* is wrong, you're still in the right place. I've got you covered. I'm going to go over how EMDR can help with all kinds of troubles. The point I am trying to make with the discussion about anxiety and depression is that distress in general is very normal to experience. If you're in distress, don't worry, you're human.

There are *so many* individuals in North America that are suffering with mental health distress, and I hope you can agree that it's an issue that is important—and I've only just discussed the tip of the iceberg. The previous statistics that I mentioned are also only considering those who have somehow reported their symptoms... how about all of those who suffer in silence?

I don't want you to be another statistic. Regardless of whether you have been diagnosed with a mental illness before, or not, I urge you to read on. The information in this book will help you take control of your life and become the director of your own "show." This is your life—nobody else's. This book will help to guide you towards how to regain complete control over your life. If you happen to catch me on a webinar, at a live event, or in-person, I can obviously help guide you in a much more thorough way. Regardless, I'm glad that you're with me now. Please keep reading.

If you're like so many of the individuals that I've treated, you may have been working on your mental health issues for years, sometimes even decades, and not experienced any real, lasting relief. Or maybe you're just starting your healing journey. Either way, don't despair, I can say this with complete conviction: Regardless of the root cause of your affliction(s), I believe the solution is EMDR.

In just a little bit, I'm going to explain how you can harness the incredible power of this approach to mental health healing. But first, I really want to hammer home what I think you may already know in your core.

YOU HAVE BEEN TRAUMATIZED

What do you think of when you hear the word "trauma"? Do you think of the survivors of war, famine or natural disasters? How about car crashes? Assault victims? What if I told you that I believe *you* are a victim of trauma?

Statistically speaking, 76% of Canadians, and 70% of Americans have reported that they've experienced a traumatic event at least once, and approximately 20% of these individuals develop Post-Traumatic Stress Disorder (PTSD) as a result (van der Kolk, 2000). In the USA, more than 13 million people are experiencing PTSD symptoms right now, and 15% of the population has reported that they have been molested, physically attacked, raped, or involved in combat (van der Kolk, 2000). Those numbers are staggering on their own, but, in my opinion, *everyone* is a trauma survivor.

Trauma interacts with, and is stored in, the brain differently than regular, non-threating experiences. As you probably know, the brain is receiving millions of stimuli in any given second—we're only aware of a few things at a time because we're selective with our attention. Under normal situations (i.e. "non-threatening" situations) the information the brain receives enters through the right side of the brain as "raw data" before being simply transferred over to the left side of the brain (over the *corpus callosum*), is coded with language and meaning, and is then stored away as long-term memory. This occurs easily because the emotional experience of the information is within our "window of tolerance" (Ogden, Minton, & Pain, 2006; Siegel, 1999).

The "window of tolerance," is the ability that an individual has, to handle a current stressor (Ogden, et. al., 2006; Siegel, 1999). It looks like this:

Window of Tolerance

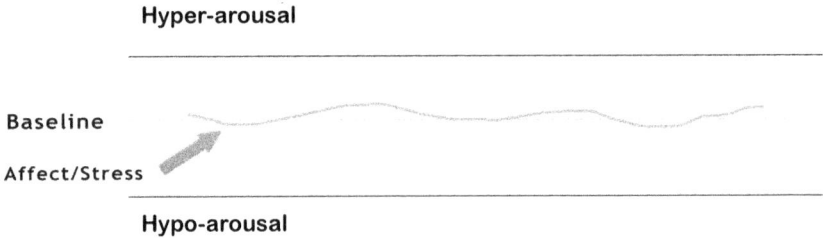

Hyper-arousal

Baseline

Affect/Stress

Hypo-arousal

Notice that the top and bottom lines create the "window"; the straight line in the middle represents "baseline"; and the wavy line (being pointed out by the arrow) represents a particular "stressor." Generally, we hover between the top and bottom of the window, and our brain processes normally. Refer to the image below (Teeradej, 2017):

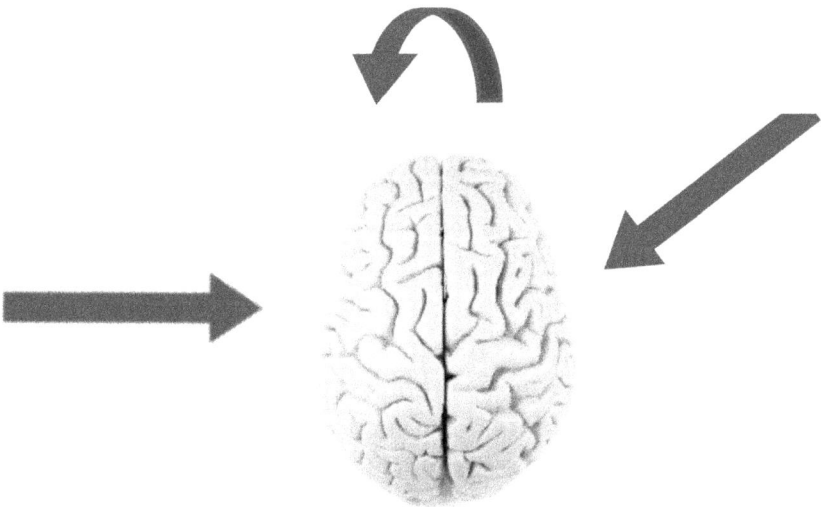

When a stressor is interpreted as being too overwhelming, the brain does not process the information in the same way, because it is generally reacting to the stressor while in "fight/flight/freeze" mode (i.e. in "reflex" or "survival" mode). The information becomes trapped in the right side of the brain and does not get processed over into the left side of the brain. The result is that the information becomes stuck as "raw" data in the right side, and becomes "misplaced," leading to maladaptive responses to triggers that, under normal circumstances, should not elicit the same response. Refer to the following diagram (Teeradej, 2017):

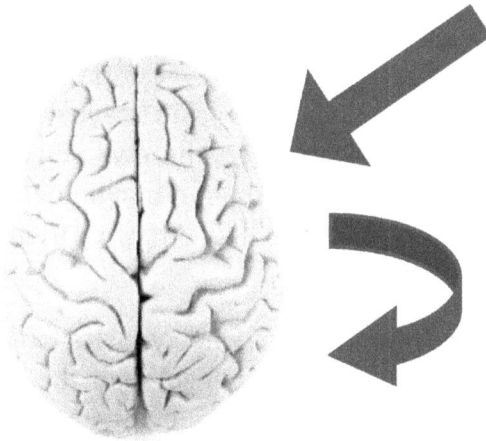

The problem with information being stuck (i.e. "unprocessed") is that the brain is not able to determine if the stressor is *currently* a threat or not, and *any* aspect of the stimuli from a stressor can remain stuck as raw data. This could be sights, sounds, textures, smells, tastes, body sensations, and even thoughts in your head at the time. You may be wondering, why this is a problem, right? Well, any of the stuck, raw data, can become material that is fair game for triggers. If you've ever had the misfortune of being triggered by a past trauma, then you can personally attest to how incredibly frustrating (and often terrifying and imprisoning) this experience can be.

What is a "trigger"? A trigger is a situation, event, person, object, or stimulus that reminds you of an earlier experience. Being triggered is not inherently negative. For example: When I smell donuts being fried, I think of my grandmother (who made the BEST sugar donuts *ever*). This brings pleasant thoughts into my mind and fills me with calmness. However, when I think I may have just spotted an ex-girlfriend where the relationship ended poorly, I instantly feel my gut dropping, and I begin to feel extremely anxious. See the difference?

Whether you know it or not, you could experience a trigger at any time. Although, unless you're experiencing one in relation to a significant source of traumatic stress, you're unlikely to recognize that you are being triggered. Here's an example of a positive trigger that I'm *sure* you've experienced: Ever notice that when you hear a song that you haven't heard for years (maybe even decades), and you can immediately remember where you were when you first heard it, or who you were with, and maybe even how you were feeling at the time? I *know* you have. That, my friend, is an example of a trigger.

You may already be aware of when you are triggered, and what sorts of things comprise your triggers—or this may be a totally new concept to you. If this is new, I invite you to start observing your day-to-day life, and try to grow your awareness as to how and when you are being triggered—both positively and negatively. It is probably easier to notice when you are being negatively triggered; but if you're looking for the positives, you'll find them.

How do you *know* you're being triggered negatively? One way is that you may instantly be reminded of an unpleasant experience, or some aspect of that experience. In this scenario, you may simply remember part of it, or the trigger may result in you feeling as though you are literally re-experiencing the traumatic event. This is called a flashback. Flashbacks can be incredibly distressing and can become destabilizing for even the most balanced individual. If this is happening for you, I urge you to remind yourself that a.) This experience is normal, and b.) That the past event is *not* happening now. I also recommend that you do whatever it takes to ensure that you are physically safe and then remind yourself *consciously* of your current safety.

Sometimes individuals are not reminded of a full-blown past memory in the visual sense. It is also possible to experience a trigger that is stored in the body as an emotional or completely somatic (physical) memory. Yes, the body itself does remember (well it's really the brain that stores the imprint of the somatic memory, but it *feels* like it's in the body). Take a second to think about how emotions are *physical* expressions, because emotions must be felt *in* the body. You can't experience joy without a smile, for instance.

Another response to being triggered is that you may begin to dissociate. Dissociation is an important topic and one that we must discuss before we go forward. What the heck is dissociation, right? "Dissociation," "trauma," "triggers" ...man it's like you're reading a psychology book, eh?

OK, all jokes aside, we all experience dissociation. Dissociation is a normal human (and animal) response to overwhelming threat. The brain shuts down its normal processing and enters survival mode processing, where the body acts automatically to preserve your safety (or sense of safety). I've also referred to this survival mode as "reflex mode" and "fight/flight/freeze."

Essentially what is happening during dissociation is that the brain and body work together to get you to safety—without your conscious effort. It's like your "autopilot" programming. Because the brain isn't processing the information under normal circumstances (within the window of tolerance) but is still absorbing millions of pieces of stimuli in any given second, the brain continues to store that information as raw data. This raw data remains stuck in the brain and is likely to become a trigger(s) in the future. However, because the brain is essentially programmed to respond to similar threats in similar ways, dissociation is far more likely in the future. It's kind of like, when I go to sleep after having survived a threat, my brain says, "Way to go, Robert, do it the same way next time."

It may be clearer if I give you an example of normal dissociation before we go into the kind that happens because of trauma. Have you ever been on a bus or train, travelling the same route as you have a million times before, and suddenly, you realize that you're at your destination stop? It's like the time went by in an instant and you can't really explain where it went? That's dissociation. It's also common for people to do this while driving to or from work, and quickly realize that they're pulling into their driveway or their work's parking lot. My personal favourite—and one that happens to me *all the time*—is walking into a room, and then being completely oblivious as to what I wanted to do in that room...UGH! These are examples of normal experiences of dissociation. And yes, it is much more dangerous if you're behind the wheel.

When dissociation occurs due to a trauma it's because of a completely different reason. Dissociation is an altered state of consciousness. *Everybody's* brain has the ability to dissociate to protect them; it either protects the individual by helping them to enter the fight-or-flight mode (and sometimes it's like another part of the individual just takes over to get the job done), or dissociation occurs as the brain produces an anaesthetic effect in reflex to prepare the organism for death. That's right, your brain has two distinct modes of dissociation: "survival mode" and "shut-down mode." In survival mode, the individual may experience dissociation as they are running from or confronting a threat, but in shut-down mode, the brain produces a neurochemical and physical response to prepare the individual to experience a painless death.

The human brain is amazing, isn't it?

Dissociation is also subjective. When I dissociate, I literally begin to experience my consciousness floating out of my body through my head, and I am aware of having the experience of staring down at myself. Simultaneously, I can feel my body experience a heavy weightiness, as I watch my body conduct itself. If you are thinking that such an experience sounds freaky, or dangerous, you're right—this sort of experience can become dangerous, and luckily this hasn't happened to me when driving. This experience has only happened a handful of times to me, but when it does happen, it *is* awfully scary.

Other people have described their dissociation to me as if they get pushed to the "back of their consciousness," and another more "dominant aspect of their psyche" comes forward to operate while they are somewhere there in the background watching. Still, others have described their dissociative experiences like they suddenly experience the world around them as somehow unreal—like they are the star in a movie, and the environment is a movie set. I've had another tell me that her dissociative experience meant the world around her looked like cardboard.

Another very commonly reported experience of dissociation is the *disconnection* of the body's *experience* of *feeling* an emotion, from the brain's *interpretation* of that feeling. This happens often when the perception of the experience of the emotions is overwhelming, and the individual does not feel capable of handling such stress, and thus "turns it off" unconsciously.

Can you see how highly subjective dissociation can be? Have you ever noticed any of these types of dissociation in your own life's experience? Don't worry if you have, as I said before, it's completely normal to dissociate. What was not normal was the original situation that you found yourself in which required that you had to dissociate to survive.

So what types of situations qualify as being "traumatic"? Well, anything has the potential to be. Here's the equation to remember:

Overwhelm + Danger (real or imagined) = Primed for Trauma

Let's pick this apart. Any time that a stressor is *too* stressful, for whatever reason, it is likely to be experienced as overwhelming. Overwhelming stress could occur due to not believing that you have the adequate coping skills to manage a given situation, when your identity is being questioned, or when you are placed in an impossible predicament and there isn't really any way *to* manage the situation (to name a few).

Take this comparison as an example of overwhelming stress: Imagine that you are a regular, average, city-slicker Joe, and while on vacation you sign up for a jungle expedition adventure. Then, somehow, you mistakenly find yourself walking into a lions' den. Seeing several hungry lions sizing you up is sure to make you feel overwhelming stress. Now compare that example to being trained as a lion tamer. Imagine that, as a lion tamer, you knowingly enter a lion's cage to teach the lion tricks, and you reward the lion with treats (*you* are not the treat!). Two very different examples of stress, right? One example would lead to overwhelming stress, the other to normal stress (that is, if you were trained as a lion tamer you would likely have a different window of tolerance for emotional arousal).

The second part of the equation is "danger" (whether it be real danger, or perceived danger). Obviously, the awareness of stumbling into a lion's den unprepared would lead one to discover quite quickly that they are in danger.

How about "perceived danger"? Perceived danger could be anything that makes one believe they are in danger. Some examples of the perception of danger could be: someone telling you that they are going to hurt you or somebody else; being shamed or publicly ridiculed; believing that you are sick and are going to die (when really, you just have the flu); and so on.

Here's an example that is far more difficult to spot: Your *idea* of "yourself" becomes challenged for some reason, and you must now adapt your identity to something else (imagine being diagnosed with an illness, or being convicted of a criminal offense, or being rejected by a loved one for some unknown reason). There are many possible examples; the most essential element of this part of the equation is that the danger (or the perception of it) is highly subjective.

Now, quite honestly, there is SO much trauma in the world, and literally (literally, literally, literally) *everyone* has experienced at least one or more traumas at this point in their lifetime. If you doubt that, can you imagine how traumatic being born is? You're nice and cozy inside your mother's womb, and then all of a sudden you're being pushed out, instantly freezing (what is "freezing"?), all kinds of things are making loud noises (these "things" are people... what the heck are "people"?), and there're bright lights (what is "light"?), and you're being grabbed and touched (what is being "touched"?); throw into the possible mix that the birthing process is complicated or that your mother has an extremely negative reaction (aside from the incredible pain that she just experienced in popping you out), and you have the basis for your first traumatic experience. And if you're wondering whether trauma can happen prior to birth, yes, it can.

In any case, the types of trauma that have been popularized in the media generally refer to the more large-T traumas (like physical assault, sexual abuse, automobile accidents, experiences of war, famine, etc.). However, small-t traumas are also a source of severe distress for many individuals—and because the "damage" is far less obvious than large-T trauma, the effects often have the host questioning their own sanity, or themselves, in some negative way.

An example of small-t trauma would be emotional abuse. Imagine that little Sue grew up in a family where the philosophy was that, "Girls are supposed to be seen, and not heard" (have you heard of that one before?). And, imagine that Sue, being a bubbly child often excited by life's little curiosities, attempts to convey her joy about seeing fireflies for the first time to her mother. Her mother, deep in conversation with her friend around the campfire, turns to little Sue and snaps at her saying, "Sue, you're such a brat. Can't you see that I don't care about that? Are you trying to give me a headache?" Sue stops jumping up and down, her shoulders begin to slouch, she becomes quiet, and then goes to sit down by herself. Notice: no punches were thrown, and Sue is in no way physically hurt—and mom doesn't even have to raise her voice.

However, do you get the sense that Sue is experiencing some emotional distress right now? Imagine that this sort of exchange (with some slight variations) occurred every day of Sue's childhood life? How do you think she would begin to feel about herself? That's right, she's likely to develop a belief about herself that she is "bad" or that she's "not important," or some other version of these.

When I was growing up, I was afraid of emotions. My parents fought occasionally, but not all *that* much. My mother became increasingly more stressed over the course of my childhood. She was stressed about our financial situation, and the growing number of tasks she had to do to keep the house clean. To her, she felt as though she was underappreciated, and basically invisible. Obviously, she was not *really* invisible to us; my father and I loved her very much (and still do)!

However, I believe now that my mother's tolerance for this emotional stress was reaching her limit of her window of tolerance and she would get angry a lot (she was probably experiencing symptoms of anxiety and depression, now that I think about it). I was so afraid to upset her—and cause her "pain." When she would yell at me, or look at me sternly, I would feel that I was somehow hurting her. The natural conclusion that I would come to was that I was bad. What kind of son is "bad" to his mother? Well, the kind that obviously is not "good enough." Remember that negative belief of mine I mentioned earlier? Doesn't "I'm bad" sound a whole lot like "I'm not good enough?" Variations of these beliefs arising from childhood are all too common.

What's often overlooked is the dominant negative core belief (or beliefs) that your parents struggle with (or struggled with, if they've gone through their healing). This is a belief that they, most likely, gathered from the trauma they endured with their own parents, and their parents with their parents, and so on. Negative core beliefs can become passed down from generation to generation—not quite as romantic as that family heirloom, eh?

What sorts of emotional trauma have you suffered? Take a moment to think about it. I bet there's something there. What about physical trauma—like physical abuse or sexual abuse? Unfortunately, these sorts of traumas happen all too frequently. Although physical and sexual abuse is not gender specific, Bessel van der Kolk (a leading psychologist in EMDR research), had reported that males are more likely to be physically assaulted, and females are more likely to be sexually assaulted (2000). While this may indeed be true, having worked with both male and female survivors of sexual abuse, the experiencing of shame that is often attached to the trauma some-times influences the underreporting of sexual trauma.

As for children, four out of five assaults on children are by their parents, and in homes that are experiencing domestic violence, the rates for child abuse are 1500% higher than in homes where domestic violence is not present (van der Kolk, 2000). These statis-tics are troubling simply because these traumas are being endured by so many, but what makes things *even worse* (if you can imagine worse) is that according to van der Kolk (2000), people who suffered severe childhood maltreatment are:

- four to twelve times more likely to develop alcoholism, depression, drug abuse, and attempt suicide
- two to four times more likely to smoke
- have 50+ sexual partners, contract an STI
- are about one and a half times more likely to be physical inactive and to be obese
- are nearly three times more likely to develop diseases like ischemic heart disease, cancer, chronic lung disease, skeletal fractures, hepatitis, stroke, diabetes, and liver disease

PTSD (Post-Traumatic Stress Disorder) is very common for indi-viduals who have experienced the unfortunate reality of childhood abuse. While you should NOT diagnose yourself, some hallmark features of PTSD are:

- being easily startled
- feeling hypervigilant (i.e. hyper-aware of surroundings)
- experiencing dissociation
- having nightmares
- enduring flashbacks
- being triggered and making attempts to consciously avoid triggers (emotionally, psychologically, somatically)
- developing negative beliefs about oneself
- low self-esteem
- and the presence of anxiety attacks

What usually flies under the radar, are the individuals who experience just a few of these symptoms and are never properly diagnosed as suffering from PTSD. These unfortunate individuals are often misdiagnosed with some other anxiety disorder, mood disorder, or sometimes even a personality disorder. While these other presentations of symptoms should not go overlooked or ignored, the failure to acknowledge the traumatic roots of these illnesses, does a grave injustice to the individual looking for help. The usual response these individuals receive is to be heavily medicated; and if they cannot afford the cost of private counselling services, they do not receive the help they need. Being treated with medication alone usually simply masks the problem, and often exacerbates the individual's suffering.

Now, I'm not saying that you are suffering from PTSD. But what I *am* absolutely stating, is that *you have undoubtedly experienced trauma in your life, and failure to properly work through the trauma is THE reason for the current distress in your life.*

Can I be blunt? Like I haven't been already, right? Have you ever heard the saying, "Just get over it?" How about, "It's in the past, move on?" What about this one: "Try focusing on all the good stuff in your life?" These sorts of statements from others become internalized into the unconscious script that we keep telling ourselves, and our inability to "move on" or to "focus on something good" generally makes us feel inadequate—like there must be something wrong with us. We cannot move on, because what we are trying to move on from is trauma.

What also does not work, is trying to simply switch your thought process to thinking positively. If you've ever tried this approach, I can almost guarantee that it hasn't worked—at least not for long. There's a reason for that. Don't worry you're not alone. It's a pet peeve of mine, and it's something that I believe is important that we focus on it next.

WHY POSITIVE THINKING DOESN'T WORK

For many years, Cognitive Psychology has provided that the antidote to negative core beliefs and statements was: "positive thinking," or "mantras," or "self-affirmations." Those terms speak to the same kind of perspective: If you are constantly saying negative things about yourself or the world around you, simply "flip the script" and start saying positive things to yourself. Makes sense, right?

This is the cure that many forms of talk-therapies and self-help books look to help individuals with. If you can figure out that those negative thoughts and beliefs don't have much merit, and that *you* are the one who is really in charge of what you're thinking, why not simply change your thoughts to be about something more positive? Many people have made millions of dollars on this concept.

Take for example, the hugely famous "Law of Attraction" and how the concept suggests that you simply need to be "thinking positive thoughts" of "already having" whatever it is you desire, and then it's supposed to manifest into your life, right? Heck, nearly all the big-name celebrities in the personal development genre use this concept in some way to make them super rich—and I have no beef with them...just their message.

The problem with their message, is that it's only half of the truth. These professional development gurus preach that you must be thinking positive thoughts to attract the results you desire. I believe this part of the message *is* true. If you are **truly** thinking positively then you **are** bound to have positive results. However, what is not being conveyed to you, is this: The message that you are saying to yourself below your consciousness, <u>is just as important, if not</u> <u>**more** important than what you consciously say to yourself</u>.

Even though you can repeat a mantra a million and one times, if you do not *believe* it at your core, or if you have another conflicting belief, then merely saying something in your head will not make it so. Because our core beliefs are so powerful, they literally comprise our identities. When you repeat something that you truly believe as being a personal fact about you, you can feel it so deeply that it feels like it's in your soul (if you believe in that sort of thing). If I believe that I am worthless (a combination of traumatic events generated the belief), and I can actually *feel* that belief in my body (a relentless, deep sadness in my gut), simply repeating the words "I am amazing" will not change my life. In fact, I believe it will make my sadness even worse as I compare how lonely I *feel* with how I believe I am *supposed* to feel.

What's the problem here? The problem is that positive beliefs on their own do not correct negative core beliefs. Negative core beliefs arise as a direct result of the effects of trauma. **The memories responsible for the generation of the belief must be dealt with *first*, prior to successfully adopting a positive belief.**

For example: Imagine that you wish to believe that you are beautiful. If you've grown up with negative experiences of people bullying you, and/or parents insulting you (such as parents telling you that you are fat) or touching you inappropriately (like pinching your belly fat), you're probably not going to grow up believing that you're beautiful. You're more likely to grow up with the belief of something like, "I am ugly," or "I'm not good enough." Merely repeating the mantra, "I'm beautiful" is not going to *feel* real. (We haven't even touched the disastrous consequences of childhood sexual abuse.) You see, the negative experiences of repeatedly being told you are fat, and your belly fat constantly being pinched (a violation of physical boundaries), over time become trauma, and these experiences remain stuck in your brain as "raw data." Every time someone looks at your torso, instead of having the (very likely) thought that they are admiring your choice of outfit today, you imagine them thinking that you are ugly.

What needs to happen instead of blindly repeating the positive statement of "I am beautiful," are focused EMDR sessions on the *distress in the* **memories** associated with the development of the belief "I am ugly." When we utilize EMDR to directly target the memories responsible for the negative belief "I am ugly," the memories become processed properly, because the distress inherent in the trauma is no longer present, and a more realistic belief can be adopted. EMDR does not implant beliefs that are not factual. If you want to believe that you are an Armenian princess, and you're not, then you are not going to be able to adopt that belief with EMDR—only a delusional psychosis will help you there!

A question I often get when someone new is inquiring into changing their negative core beliefs through working with me is, "So, what's the timeline with EMDR?" Hard to say. I can say this quite confidently though: It's much less than with regular talk therapy. Other forms of therapy work by addressing the symptoms, not the root cause.

Psychodynamic therapies work by helping you build awareness of where the belief first came about, and perhaps why you keep choosing to act in accordance with that belief; but the focus is on building self-awareness and helping you to outline better alternative choices.

Cognitive Behavioural Therapy (CBT) works by helping you to try and become a critical thinker about yourself, assessing the "evidence" for the facts of your "ugliness" and challenging them; then CBT, like other cognitive therapies, might have you conduct homework assignments about different choices you could adopt in the future.

EMDR, by contrast, doesn't focus on the symptoms at all—it focuses on the memories responsible for the symptoms. And when the memories are desensitized and reprocessed, the symptoms simply disappear. The human system has no need for symptoms without a cause ("Symptoms Without a Cause"...this could be the name of a hit pop song, don't you think?).

In response to the question about timelines: Regular talk therapy may take individuals years to show any improvement, while EMDR can take a handful of sessions. Pretty amazing, eh?

So, when that super successful and rich personal development guru asks you to think positively, and, no matter how hard you try, there is still that lingering voice in the back of your mind that says, "Yeah, but..."—that's your clue to go deeper. What's the belief that is blocking you from *truly feeling the validity of that positive thought* that the guru is trying to get you to adopt? When you can identify that, then you can remove it, so that you *can* follow what the rich and successful idol is trying to get you to adopt.

OK...SO WHAT DO I DO NOW?

Great question. As per the title of this book, "You NEED Therapy," I'm going to absolutely **_BEG_** you to seriously consider Eye Movement Desensitization and Reprocessing (EMDR) therapy. I'm telling you, nothing even comes close to comparison. There are literally thousands of people (maybe even hundreds of thousands of people—possibly millions) who have gone to therapy for *years* and have repeatedly shared the same story with their therapist (or likely several therapists over the course of their treatment careers), and not really found complete relief—not real lasting relief, anyway. As per the discussion in the last chapter, this is because the traditional therapies don't focus on the *real root* of the problem—only the symptoms or environmental situations. EMDR focuses upon the roots of the distress—the memories responsible for keeping the distress present.

Traditional psychotherapy teaches individuals to gather awareness of what's really going on for them, and even why one feels the way they do. It also trains individuals to think differently and practice better coping techniques when distressed. Unfortunately, while the individual has learned how to handle the distress better and cope more efficiently, the distress still remains present. So, as soon as a new scenario triggers that original distress, the problem returns.

EMDR <u>entirely removes</u> the distress associated with the memories responsible for why you would feel distressed in the first place. When the distress is removed, and the memory is reprocessed in a more realistic way, there is no reason to feel the distress anymore in that situation.

Imagine that you have a knife in your leg. Every movement is painful, and you can no longer enjoy life as you used to. Traditional psychotherapy (Psychodynamic, Cognitive Behavioural Therapy, etc.) would teach you how to identify the pain in your leg and how to position your body more effectively so that you place less strain on the leg. It may even teach you how to induce a bit of calm during particularly stressful days (like if someone bumps your leg). Even Existential Psychotherapy (my previous favourite form of psychotherapy) would teach you to take responsibility for the situation you found yourself in, and to try and find meaning within this dreadful scenario. EMDR would be as if you removed the knife entirely. It would hurt first indeed—there's no way around feeling the pain of removing that knife from your leg—but after it has been removed, your leg would begin to heal on its own, and there would be no reason to continue to feel the pain.

Take me for example. I had gone to three different therapists over the course of five years for several reasons. One reason was to work on my self-esteem (i.e. that negative core belief of "I'm worthless"—although it was before I really understood that I *had* that negative core belief); another, was to address my addictions and self-sabotaging behaviours; another reason, was to help me work through my issues related to women, and my own sexuality. And I'll say this with complete honesty and conviction: My therapists were amazing to me, and they are really, *really* good at what they do. I learned a lot about myself, like how I could handle myself differently, and what choices I could make in the future. But, I never got rid of the feelings underlying those patterns and situations that kept repeating themselves. I was on a vicious cycle of the negative core belief "I'm not good enough," and conducting self-sabotaging behaviours where I ultimately reinforced that belief for myself (with an extra dose of guilt or shame, I might add).

This is the heart of what EMDR therapy is about. EMDR works by changing how your brain stores the negative memories responsible for how you feel about yourself and the world. If the memories are no longer distressing, then there is no reason to maintain the negative core beliefs as such, and you are free to adopt a more positive and empowering perspective on that same memory. Quite simply, an original source of distress and disempowerment could become a source of strength and confidence.

Since the time of EMDR's conception—which was all the way back in 1987—there has been numerous studies conducted on the effectiveness of EMDR. The American Psychiatric Association, the World Health Organization, the U.S. Department of Veterans Affairs and Department of Defense, the U.S. Department of Health and Human Services, the Dutch National Steering Committee, and the National Institute for Clinical Excellence, and many other international health agencies, all recognize EMDR as an *effective* form of treatment (EMDR International Association, 2017; Shapiro, 2001). When you notice that these prestigious organizations are located throughout the globe, it demonstrates the universality of this approach—it doesn't matter what language one speaks, or what culture one is in: EMDR is effective.

EMDR is also a controlled discipline. The EMDRIA (EMDR International Association), provides structured trainings all over the world, and requires that practitioners constantly upgrade their craft to remain affiliated with them. EMDRIA helps to provide grant money for those interested in scientifically researching EMDR and provides access to peer-reviewed journals that both support EMDR treatment as well as those studies that didn't support the results of EMDR. As a professional organization, this level of transparency demonstrates their commitment to an unbiased opinion of EMDR to the public. Anyone can access the studies, but not just "anyone" can practice EMDR.

I absolutely love and **respect** this form of treatment. When I first began my counselling career, I practiced from an existentialist perspective. This meant that I was focused upon empathizing with how my client viewed their world and helping that individual to cultivate the courage to accept their current reality. I would then attempt to help motivate that client to take responsibility for what they were doing (or not doing!) to manifest the reality that they truly wanted for their life. Essentially, I would help these individuals point out to themselves how they were living "inauthentically," and help them take steps to live *more* "authentically." This form of therapy is still intriguing to me, and it sounds totally fantastic, right? Who wouldn't want to live in accordance with their true authentic reality? Well, I ran into some problems with this way of thinking about psychotherapy.

Firstly, I was unaware as to the full meaning of the word, "trauma." I simply was not educated to view trauma in the widest sense—mainly that all sorts of things could be considered traumatic for an individual (remember the concepts of large-T trauma and small-t trauma?). This ignorance on my behalf meant that I was not really helping my clients create lasting change, merely temporary ones. For these individuals, therapy was like freshly cutting the lawn to remove the flower heads from a patch of dandelions, before we knew it, a new batch of dandelions sprouted up next session.

Secondly, for some individuals, my therapeutic task was seemingly insurmountable because of the extent of their suffering. How could I have corrected the effects of a lifetime of psychological, emotional, and physical abuse (in some cases)? Trying to help some of these clients was like trying to take down a 300-year-old redwood tree with a spoon. We both knew that we would have to be in it for the long haul, and even still, therapy had no guarantees.

Eventually, I got frustrated with the growing sense of professional inadequacy. Not only did I feel like I was not *really* helping my clients, I was getting extremely burnt out in the process. Two years of treating trauma clients with talk therapy was making me depressed (not to mention vicariously traumatized).

It was on one fateful day, when I returned home from a particularly draining day (I had about four or five 90-minute sessions with individuals who certainly had their [un]fair share of trauma), when I thought, "I can't keep doing this." I realized that if I continued at the rate I was going—or that treatment was going, I wouldn't be able to sustain myself. I'd be fried before my 31st birthday! Not only that, I considered how my clients must have been feeling—it's great to have someone hear them and be with them in the "mud," but how would they ever get their tires onto dry land?

It was then that I remembered sitting in one of my classes for my master's degree in counselling psychology and writing down "EMDR" as a treatment for trauma. It was one of those things where it wasn't even a full thought; it was like a half thought that I wrote down in one of my book margins and just about completely forgot about.

I can't even remember how I came across his teaching, but I ended up in a basic training course for EMDR (an EMDRIA accredited course offered by the BC School of Professional Counselling) taught by Dr. Marshall Wilensky. I do remember sitting in his class (in the front row), having no expectations at all. I was just there to get a little bit more information about how to treat trauma—and boy was I in for a life-changing experience! Dr. Wilensky changed my life. His sense of humour and his laugh caught me off-guard and neutralized what seemed like insanely bold claims for trauma treatment. He spoke of individuals healing PTSD in his office in mere sessions—SESSIONS! Not *years*!

I was intrigued, but a little hesitant. I had been working with several people for several years and none of them spontaneously improved (more like they wanted to spontaneously combust!). Then he demonstrated what EMDR "looked" like—a hand waving back and forth in front of someone's face. I thought to myself, "When is the break? I'm out of here as soon as I go for lunch. This is a waste of my time. This guy's crazy!" EMDR looked like hypnosis for crazy people.

Then Dr. Wilensky showed some video clips of actual sessions (of people who consented to being recorded), and I watched how the symptoms of trauma for these individuals literally *disappeared* before my eyes. I couldn't believe it. WOW. A few waves of this guy's hand in front of this woman's face, and she no longer is distressed with the death of her husband? Then there were the video recordings of the founder of EMDR, Dr. Francine Shapiro, as well as several other clinicians who demonstrated how they were eliminating the distress that their clients were experiencing in similar amounts of time; and let me tell you, these individuals were not faking it. Example after example went by, and eventually I thought, "Well…seeing *is* believing, isn't it?"

Slowly, but surely, the examples kept mounting, and my curiosity, as well as my professional faith, mounted in response. I remember thinking that this "hand-waving" treatment was as close to a "Jesus miracle" as I would ever see. I was in. I "drank the Kool-Aid®…"

Now I don't expect for you to be "all in" with regards to EMDR treatment as I was after I was first introduced to this revolutionary approach to therapy. I certainly don't want you to simply believe in the power of EMDR because my mind was "blown" by Dr. Wilensky. I want you to believe in this approach to therapy because it works. And that's what I hope to share with you in the next chapter.

SO...EMDR WORKS RIGHT?

YES! When I first began to utilize what I had learned in my EMDR basic training course with my current clients, I was amazed at the results. Check out the following examples of successes from my own practice. Afterwards, I'll also provide you with results from published scientific journals that prove EMDR's effectiveness.

One client—let's call him John—had been suffering from intense bouts of rage related to suffering from being molested by an older boy when he was very young. John was actively cutting himself, and even tried to commit suicide in the middle of our treatment. It had been two years since we started, and I felt like I was getting nowhere with him, in fact, it felt like he was getting worse. Then I began to utilize EMDR with John, and in a matter of three or four sessions, John went from absolutely loathing the thought of his abuser, to believing that he could have a civil conversation with him, and even *forgive* his abuser if he ran into him. *Are you serious?!*

After that trauma, John and I worked on his feelings of isolation, agoraphobia, and social anxiety stemming from his suppressed transsexual gender identity. In just a few more months, John completed therapy, feeling more confident and balanced then he ever had before. Two years of talk therapy or a few months of EMDR? Hmmm...

Another of my past clients, let's call him Sheldon, was seeing me for about the same amount of time (weekly sessions for at least two years, which translated into over 100 sessions). Sheldon is an elderly gentleman, who was suffering from blackouts, extreme

PTSD symptoms, amnesia-like memory issues, rage, and a consistently deteriorating marriage to his partner. Sheldon's past was a very traumatic one. He suffered from neglectful parenting, an instance of rape in his teenage years, involuntarily being admitted to a psychiatric facility which would attempt to "cure him of his homosexuality" with repeated electro-convulsive shock-therapy (*can anyone say, "***torture***"?*). After that experience, Sheldon went on to becoming absorbed by a cult who committed further torture on him. Did I mention that during our two-year therapeutic relationship, Sheldon struggled mightily with suicidal ideation—yeah, no kidding, right? The fact that he was still alive and could smile at me, crack jokes with me, and even remembered my birthday, inspired the heck out of me.

After receiving about three months of EMDR (about 12 sessions lasting 90 minutes each), Sheldon was no longer suicidal. He didn't experience PTSD symptoms anymore; his memory improved; he was confident and assertive (sometimes he could be a little bit on the verbally aggressive side, but hey, who's perfect, right?). He no longer had nightmares, he didn't black out, and he created a three-way romantic relationship with his partner so that both he and his partner were happy. How about *that*?

Then I worked with a young woman, named Brianna (Brianna provided me with consent to share her testimony), who, as an artist, suffered from bouts of creative "painter's block." Brianna was depressed, and even suffered from blurred vision—a dissociative result of her depression. Brianna worked with me for nine sessions (one session was devoted to history-taking and intake procedures) before she no longer was depressed, her vision restored, and creative drive replenished! Her relationship even improved, as she and her partner moved away together.

Here's Brianna's testimony:

> *Before I started my sessions with Robert, I was in a depression that had followed me on and off for years.*

My mental health issues were preventing me from being able to pursue my ambitions and think clearly. I was also experiencing symptoms of depersonalization and blurred vision due to my depression that made it hard for me to relate to my surroundings.

After a couple months of frequent EMDR sessions, I was back to a place of stability, which eventually lead to complete mental and visual clarity. I have been depression-free for one year now, despite many traumatic events taking place involving death and sickness of family members, which typically would have triggered a depressive episode. Robert is kind, patient and understanding, and I would highly recommend his service for anyone dealing with symptoms of depression.

(Brianna K.)

I'm happy to report that nearly two years later, Brianna's symptoms of depression have not returned, and she is looking onward to her upcoming marriage and the next chapter of her life.

Jane had come to me after experiencing panic attacks and was struggling with issues of depression and perfectionism (all stemming from a childhood where she faced impossibly unrealistic expectations). Jane also struggled with alcohol and drug abuse, an eating disorder, and suffered from the shame she carried after being sexually molested. She also experienced grief related to the deaths of several close individuals to her.

During the intake session, we quickly identified that Jane's most dominant negative belief about herself, was that she was "not good enough."

We targeted all the necessary memories related to her neglectful childhood and adult life that fed into the belief, "I am not good enough." After three 90-minute sessions, Jane was free from the grips of her perfectionism, and she was fully aware that she indeed *is* good enough.

Thomas struggled with cocaine abuse and came to me for help because he was on the brink of losing his job (a good one too!). Thomas's addiction stemmed from his belief that he was "worthless." After six sessions of targeting the memories related to his negative belief and neutralizing his triggers for using cocaine, Thomas no longer had urges to use the drug (even in scenarios where he would normally feel unable to control himself) and was then able to fully embrace his positive self-worth.

Sven came to me struggling with feeling invisible when he and his partner would begin to fight. Sven felt that he was "unimportant." Every time he attempted to stand up to his partner, he experienced an overwhelming anxiety and would begin to cry. Sven was tired of feeling afraid of confrontation.

We identified Sven's "root memories" associated with the belief, "I am unimportant," and after just five 90-minute sessions, Sven was changed. He was sitting taller on the couch in front of me, he effectively communicated with his partner about his feelings, and felt strong enough to leave his romantic relationship after determining that his emotional needs weren't being met.

John, a high-ranking and widely-appreciated individual in his field of work (his work is protected for privacy purposes), came to me struggling with his intimacy in his relationship and feelings of professional inadequacy (i.e. feeling that he always needed to prove himself, despite being at the top in his professional category). We worked together for just a handful of three-hour, extended sessions before John reached a new level of self-awareness, was proud of his professional competency, and clearly improved his level of trust and intimacy with his partner.

These cases are just a select few amongst many. Anyone who is serious about working with EMDR and complies with the course of their treatment can expect results. I share these examples with you not to boast, but rather, to show you the results of *real* people who have undergone EMDR treatment, and successfully changed their lives for good. EMDR is my calling: *Real* people with *real* problems getting *real* help.

You may be thinking, "OK, Robert. Those are splendid examples, but your experience must surely be an anomaly. There's no way that these results are typical." If you're wondering something along those lines, I certainly can't blame you for your hesitation. Here are some examples from published research studies:

- In one study, of 80 patients with serious mental trauma who were treated with EMDR over just three 90-minute sessions, 80% of these patients reported the absence of symptoms for PTSD, and 15 months later their results improved (Croitoru, 2014)!

- A study by Gauhar (2016) showed that EMDR yielded a 95% effectiveness rate for treating depression, compared to a 40-50% effectiveness rate for treating depression that combined Cognitive Behavioural Therapy with medication (the most common method of treatment for depression to date). Furthermore, Gauhar showed that it only took six to eight sessions of EMDR to show noticeable improvement.

- A U.S. National Comorbidity Survey published their findings that the "depression relapse rate" for those treated with CBT was between 50% and 80%, compared to the "depression relapse rate" for those treated with EMDR as being 0% (Gauhar, 2014)!

- For years, Mark Grant has been writing on and studying the benefits of utilizing EMDR to reduce and alleviate the symptoms of pain, including many forms of chronic pain. Grant's findings indicate that there is beginning to be more solid evidence that EMDR is an effective approach to eliminating symptoms of chronic pain (Grant & Threlfo, 2002; Grant, 2015).

- Results of eight studies by Natha and Daiches (2014), showed that EMDR was "extremely effective" in reducing PTSD symptoms following natural disasters (treatment times ranged from only one to eight sessions).

- Chemtob, Nakashima, Hamada, and Carlson conducted a study where 32 children diagnosed with PTSD were provided with three 90-minute EMDR sessions following their survival of Hurricane Iniki (all children were reported to have no change in symptoms for almost four years prior to the use of EMDR). Results of the study indicated that 56% of participants no longer met the criteria for PTSD (Shapiro, 2001).

- Bleich, Kotler, Kutz, and Shalev found that EMDR is one of three methods recommended for the treatment of terror victims (Shapiro, 2001).

- The French National Institute of Health and Medical Research found that EMDR was a treatment of choice for trauma victims (Shapiro, 2001).

- Marcus, Marquis, and Sakai studied 67 individuals receiving standard hospital care (individual Cognitive, Psychodynamic, or Behavioural therapy, with possible group therapy), and discovered that after only three sessions, 50% of EMDR participants no longer met PTSD criteria (compared to only 20% treated with the hospital's standard care). At the end of treatment (six sessions of EMDR versus 11 standard care) 77% of the EMDR group no longer met PTSD criteria compared to 50% of the control group; and, furthermore, at the three and the six-month follow-up, EMDR effects were maintained or improved (Shapiro, 2001).

- Both initial uncontrolled and controlled studies have found that EMDR can be useful to treat specific phobias within a limited number of sessions (De Jongh, Broeke, & Renssen, 1999).

- A study by Aslani, Miratashi, and Aslani demonstrated that EMDR is effective to reduce the physiological symptoms of speech anxiety as well as increase the speaker's confidence (2013).

- When used in combination with emotionally-oriented interventions, EMDR has been found effective in boosting treatment responses and has significantly improved outcomes of couple's therapy (Protinsky, H., Sparks, J, & Flemke, K., 2001).

- There have been numerous controlled studies that have indicated that 77-90% of civilians diagnosed with PTSD have experienced complete recovery within three 90-minute sessions (Shapiro, 2001).

There are many more studies that showcase the powerful healing ability that EMDR has for treating a wide range of problematic issues.

Originally, EMDR was used to treat PTSD in U.S. war veterans and it proved to be incredibly effective. Soon afterwards, studies emerged to demonstrate that EMDR is effective to treat all kinds of different symptom constellations, disorders, and problematic behaviour. Here is a (non-exhaustive) list of what I've found EMDR to be effective to treat:

- Trauma and PTSD (e.g., childhood abuse, veterans, police officers, first responders, physical or sexual assault victims, workplace accidents, near-death experiences, medical illnesses, hospital traumas, etc.)

- Phobias and Panic Disorders (e.g., social anxiety, [fear of: flying, animals, public speaking, etc.], panic attacks, agoraphobia, etc.)

- Depression (e.g., episodes and disorders, suicidality, etc.)

- Excessive Grief (e.g., loss of loved ones, career, changes in athletic ability, changes in and new diagnosis of health conditions, etc.)

- Survivors of Natural Disasters (e.g., hurricanes, floods, tornadoes, forest fires, etc.)
- Addiction (e.g., alcohol, drugs, gambling, sexual compulsions, video games, T.V., smartphones, etc.)
- Sexual Dysfunctions (e.g., impotence, premature ejaculation, etc.)
- Performance Anxiety (e.g., surgeons, sports players, musicians, actors, etc.)
- Dissociative Disorders (e.g., DID, other dissociative disorders, etc.)
- Somatoform Disorders (e.g., body dysmorphic disorders, chronic pain, etc.)
- Eating Disorders (e.g., anorexia, bulimia, binge eating, etc.)
- Personality Disorders (e.g., narcissism, borderline, histrionic, etc.)
- And almost anything else, except for disorders stemming from a biological orientation (like a brain injury, for example)

EMDR is such a respected form of trauma treatment, that it was even used to treat the survivors of: the Oklahoma City bombing, the Columbine Massacre, 9/11, and natural disasters in the West and Far East (Croitoru, 2014). In fact, there are many EMDR practitioners who travel the world to provide emergency trauma treatment after large-scale trauma has occurred (think of it as "**EMDR** Without Borders").

Since the development and preference of many clients to engage in online treatment, EMDR therapists are even beginning to take advantage of providing the incredible healing abilities of EMDR for individuals all over the world, often from the comfort of their home office!

If you are still not entirely convinced of the healing power of EMDR, I can't blame you. The claims made from EMDR practitioners, even if they *are* supported by research, are rather bold. I don't expect for you to simply believe me because I've taken the time to write some of them down. Do your own research and form your own opinions. *Please feel free to check out my website* (www.GrigoreCounselling. com) *where you can find more information and a list of valuable free handouts.*

Assuming you *are* becoming more and more intrigued by this EMDR stuff, a very common question I receive when I'm doing my live events is: "If EMDR is really so powerful, and well-researched, why is it not the <u>default</u> form of psychotherapy?" This is a good question, and one that I can only speculate about.

As you may already be aware, many healthcare systems in western nations utilize psychopharmacology as part of the medical model of treatment. In my opinion, medication is indeed useful for some individuals, but is seldom the answer to real transformation. I believe psychopharmacological treatment can help *some* people get over the "hump" of a particularly dreadful time in their life, or even help to numb the pain for a brief period (such as when there is a highly-elevated risk for suicide). The important words are: "A brief period." In most cases, medication should *not* be used long-term.

How does the use of medication tie into my beliefs as to why EMDR isn't the default form of psychotherapy? I wonder if the mega multi-billion-dollar pharmacological industry has anything to do with the standard of combining medication with talk therapy?

As I've mentioned before, talk therapy often takes quite a bit longer than EMDR therapy, and if an individual is on medication while engaging in talk therapy (or worse, isn't even *in* therapy), then the pharmacological industry stands to make quite a bit more profit off that individual. According to the Institute of Health Economics (2010), the average cost of psycho-pharmaceuticals per person in Canada was $84.80 in 2010. And considering that the population of Canada in the year 2010, was 34,126,173 (PopulationPyramid. net, 2010), that means that the Canadian pharmaceutical industry made CAD $2,893,899,470.40. My phone almost started smoking when I entered those numbers in the calculator app! And considering that the population in Canada has risen to 36.29 million in 2016, I'm not even going to try and calculate that because I need my phone. If the individual is healed within a matter of months instead of years, who's going to be most upset by that person's speedy health recovery?

Next, there's no question that talk therapy has been psychology's "Golden Child" since the late 1800s, when it was first conceptualized as a treatment discipline by Sigmund Freud, as "Psychoanalysis." EMDR has only been around since the '80s—three decades is quite a while now, but it's nothing compared to two centuries. There are many clinical practitioners who still deny the efficacy of EMDR, regardless of the growing amount of controlled scientific research studies. For those not willing to accept the research and who are fighting to hang on to their accustomed way of conducting therapy, the old cliché applies—you can't teach an old dog new tricks.

When I first took my basic training in EMDR, I noticed that there were psychologists and psychiatrists in attendance, amongst others who have been practicing psychotherapy for quite some time. A very common complaint from these individuals was that they felt that the EMDR protocol was too strict, and they felt that their clients would not receive the same level of empathy, unconditional positive regard, and gentleness that they were used to receiving. This is a logical complaint to me because the EMDR protocols can seem quite strict at first, and the way that EMDR is conducted is very different than talk therapy.

However, from my experience of conducting EMDR, I still provide my clients with *loads* of empathy, unconditional positive regard, and gentleness (when appropriate). These qualities of interpersonal interaction can be provided with very few words and are capable of being conveyed with intonations of the voice. So, while I may not launch into a monologue about how I believe my client may be feeling when they share something with me, I'm certain that 99% of my clients feel that I am empathizing with them. And moreover, when my clients start to see the amazing results this type of therapy has, pretty much everything else becomes secondary to them!

Finally, my EMDR sessions are structured in such a way that I provide approximately 15 minutes at the start of each session for updates, strengthening our therapeutic bond, and establishing the direction for the remainder of our session time. I spend at least five to 15 minutes at the end of each session to ensure that my clients are well-grounded and can contain the emotional material that was just expressed—this is often very much appreciated, and works to improve our bond, especially as we debrief the session (this is a wonderful time for empathy).

If I had to respond to the professionals who found that the EMDR protocol was too strict for them and they felt like they were losing the "art" of the craft, I would encourage them to challenge the way they view psychotherapy.

Now, I'll also say that I don't force my clients to desensitize via the EMDR protocols every session—no, sometimes clients *need* to have a talk session. This could be for several reasons, such as:

- They need to connect verbally with someone to receive the validation they don't get outside of therapy
- Or perhaps the last EMDR desensitization session still needs to be further debriefed
- Or there was a change in the client's personal situation

My clients "drive the bus," I'm just there "with the map." Since I can't say I was practicing anywhere near as long as some other clinicians at the time I started learning how to conduct EMDR, I suppose I could say that I was just lucky to be young enough to learn a new trick!

So, in response to the question of why EMDR may not be the standard form of psychotherapy, there isn't one all-encompassing answer. The insistence for adhering to the medical model for health treatment in the West could have something to do with it (insurance companies can be the worst for this sometimes), capitalism perhaps, or it could be that some psychotherapists are not ready to alter their approach of conducting psychotherapy. And let's face it: There will *always* be some important reasons for engaging in talk therapy.

My hope for the field of psychotherapy is that everyone is trained in EMDR, and they can choose when to utilize this approach. Just like we, as disciplined EMDR practitioners, ensure that we provide our clients with a wide assortment of tools, therapists should also have an ever-expanding toolkit filled with the latest interventions and techniques. It's only fair and responsible that we practice that way.

I'll tell you this if you're starting to seriously consider EMDR therapy: Find the right therapist. I will provide you with some tips as to how to narrow down your search and identify who would be the best therapist for you, in a later section, entitled, *"How to Get the Most Out of Your EMDR Therapy."* For now, let's talk a bit more about exactly *how* EMDR works.

HOW EMDR WORKS:
THE AIP MODEL OF CHANGE

The Adaptive Information Processing (AIP) Model of Change is the core guiding principle of how EMDR therapy works. AIP is somewhat like the underlying principle of Abraham Maslow's Hierarchy of Needs. Maslow was a revolutionary psychologist who contributed many great pieces of work to the psychology world. Perhaps his most widely-known contribution was his 1943 development of a theory of human development called the Hierarchy of Needs (McLeod, 2017).

The Hierarchy of Needs can be thought of as a triangle with categories of "needs" that every individual has. Each need is layered upon each other, with the most basic of needs starting at the bottom, and each level above consisting of more advanced, specific needs. See the diagram below, for a picture of Abraham Maslow's Hierarchy of Needs (McLeod, 2017):

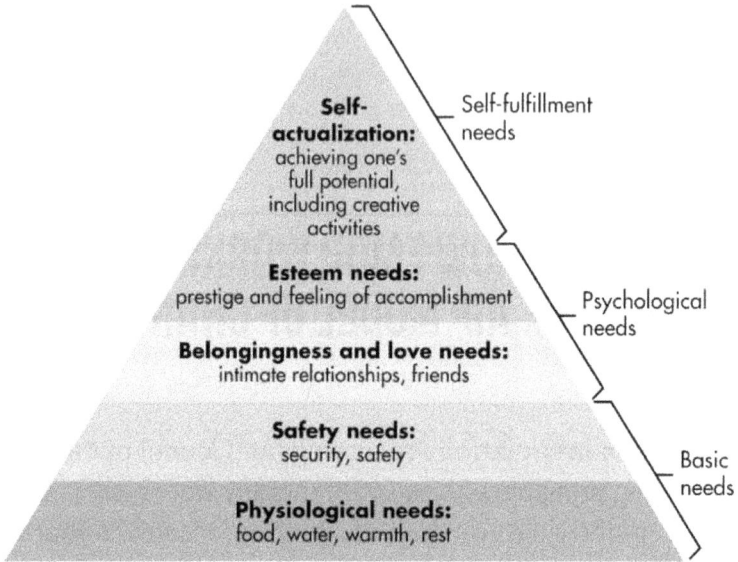

As you may notice, Maslow believed the individual's needs begin with the more basic of "physiological needs": food, water, warmth, and rest. The next basic needs are "safety needs," and include: security and safety (i.e. to not be in danger). The individual then requires that certain psychological needs are met: "belongingness and love" (intimate relationships and friends); and "esteem needs" (prestige and feeling of accomplishment). Finally, if all the needs heretofore have been met, the individual is able to move into fulfilling their ultimate need: "self-actualization" (the achieving of one's full potential, with an emphasis on creative activities).

Maslow believed that every individual maintains the ability for self-actualization, and indeed, are moving towards this self-fulfillment need. However, any failure to move upwards in the triangular hierarchy, means that one of the foundational needs below it is blocked or unmet (McLeod, 2017).

Similarly, to Maslow's Hierarchy of Needs, Shapiro's Adaptive Information Processing (AIP) Model of Change suggests that the individual maintains a natural inclination to grow, heal, and self-actualize. Any failure to move in this stated direction is an indication that the individual has encountered some sort of block (i.e. trauma) and cannot move forward until it is resolved. However, if the block is addressed and removed, the individual's innate capacity to heal means that they simply continue to grow and to self-actualize.

A previous therapist of mine once described the healing process of EMDR as the following: Just like your leg is primed to begin healing if it encounters any physical trauma (i.e. you break it), so too does your brain naturally begin to heal if it encounters any psychological trauma. Your leg is naturally able to heal on its own once a doctor sets your bones together in a cast (otherwise it may begin to heal unevenly). The same can be said about how your brain is primed to heal naturally, but you need a trained EMDR practitioner to help you set your brain's focus on the proper course.

Remember, whatever it is that you have encountered and there-fore, had to suffer through, the critical point that I cannot stress enough is this:

> You have the ability to heal yourself of any psychological trauma, regardless of the magnitude of distress you feel; you simply need to choose and trust in the right EMDR therapy and psychotherapist, and then follow through with it. Believe me, even if you don't think it's possible to be helped—you can be.

Since I have been using EMDR as my primary treatment model, I have had the privilege to help individuals heal from traumas that, quite honestly, I don't think I could have endured if I were them. Once the blocks were removed and the original traumas were eliminated from their brain and body as being "traumatic," these individuals healed naturally. Not only did these clients experience the elimination of previously distressing symptoms, their lives improved to a completely new level that some of them never even envisioned!

So, imagine that EMDR doesn't only have to be about ridding you of the symptoms of your ailment, it can be about attaining a higher, more vibrant version of yourself. Pretty amazing, right? If this can happen for so many others who have undergone this form of healing, *why not you*?

You may be asking, "What if my trauma wasn't *that bad*, and I'm still suffering? Does that mean there's something wrong with me?" Or, "Am I just weak?" Simple answer: No.

There's nothing wrong with you, even if you are aware that there hasn't been an *entire* childhood of several severe large-T trauma experiences, you are still allowed to receive trauma treatment. It simply means that, as a regular human being, your system receives inputs from outside (your environment) or from inside (within yourself), and codes them based upon the algorithms (i.e. core beliefs) that it grew up with. Simply put, as a child you learned how to make meaning out of the environment and your place in it, and as events happened to you, your brain attempted to categorize those events as best it could—and it couldn't do it any other way for you (your responses were basically rigged).

For example, because I was an only child growing up within a middle-class family household and I suffered with weight problems, my core beliefs were that I was fat, alone, and therefore worthless. I never got to experience life as a child with real siblings—no matter how great my cousins and friends were. I always felt that other people were playing real-life baseball every Sunday in their backyard with other kids, while I played baseball on a video game system and ate potato chips and macaroni and cheese.

When I was bullied in school, instead of laughing it off and responding with some quick remark, I internalized their statements of ridicule as truth and then withdrew into myself. Their insults were not seen as insults to me at the time. To me, their words were evidence that I *was* ugly, disgusting, not good enough, and therefore, worthless. These beliefs were further reinforced when I encountered experiences in my adulthood that *felt* the same as how I felt during these earlier experiences. The result was that these adult experiences confirmed my childhood beliefs of myself and became further entrenched in my unconscious!

Notice that I did not mention that I suffered from chronic physical or sexual abuse, or that I suffered from a debilitating illness throughout my childhood, or that I grew up with an alcoholic family member. Merely experiencing several instances that provided me with (false) evidence of my ugliness, and loneliness was enough to generate the negative core belief that "I am not good enough" and therefore "I am worthless."

Regardless of how severe or "tame" you believe your traumas were in your childhood, they *are* relevant. It doesn't matter if Peter down the street had a worse childhood than you did, or if you *are* Peter—in both cases, you are entitled to heal your trauma.

It's amazing the kinds of things that children "try on" from others and begin to wear for decades. The funny thing with children is that they are far more receptive to statements made from others, not just from their parents, but also from other adults, their peers, and the media. Children are sensitive—all children absorb messages from their world—it's how they adapt and grow. Because you've absorbed messages from your world during childhood and are now dealing with a negative core belief (or two, or ten!), this is simply a sign that you're operating like a *normal* human being. Normal human beings *are* traumatized beings.

Since children are likely to adopt belief systems from those around them, they unknowingly carry these perspectives out into the world with them. Because it's so ingrained in them, they may not know that any other reality exists. But since you know that core belief systems run underneath the surface and influences patterns of behaviour and thought, you might also start to suspect that there might be a way to change them, regardless of how early they were learned. Maybe you might even guess that these early belief systems can be eliminated... After all, there must be a reason why I keep bringing up the concept of core beliefs, right?!

Because of the Adaptive Information Processing model of change (the "heart" of EMDR), we are primed to be able to properly code and adopt new patterns of beliefs. This occurs when the original traumatic memory or memories responsible for the negative belief system is targeted directly, and then desensitized. Afterwards, we are free to adopt belief systems regarding those memories that are far more accurate.

A key point to stress—one that many clients struggle with initially—is that EMDR does *not* eliminate aspects of the individual's experience that are necessary for survival. This means that someone could not eliminate the ability to become stressed or anxious, as anxiety is a necessary component of survival. Likewise, the *ability* to dissociate is not something that could be eliminated with EMDR, but the tendency to experience dissociation *due* to *specific* traumatic triggers *could* be eliminated.

A second point is that EMDR is factually-based. This means that EMDR will not desensitize and reprocess information that is a fact. Now, there is a *significant* difference between remembering a "fact" and the distress associated with that fact. For example, when I remember the time I broke my right foot, I do not currently experience distress or pain with the memory—even though at the time it certainly hurt. See that difference? Likewise, memories about things that occurred that would elicit appropriate emotional responses will continue to elicit emotional responses. However, EMDR will help to eliminate the *suffering* of those emotional responses.

Here's another example: When I imagine how the loneliness of being an only child who was bullied a lot during childhood felt, I experience a feeling of sadness inside of me (it would be natural to feel this sort of empathic response for a child who was bullied), however, I do not experience the overwhelming negative cognition that I am worthless. Nor do I experience the sensation of "dropping" in the pit of my stomach when I remember feeling alone. I can think of those bullies with sympathy now, as I imagine the sorts of family trauma they might have been dealing with. They were empowered to disempower me, that way they gathered control over at least one area in their life. Some even, may have been trying to "toughen me up" because they *liked me*—and that's how they learned to show affection.

Do you see the difference between feeling emotions for a memory and feeling *distressed* by the memory? I can empathize with the experience that my younger child-self endured, but I do not feel *upset* by the feelings.

Here's my take away point about the AIP Model of Change: *you already have the ability to heal your problems, all you need is to eliminate the roadblocks to your natural growth.* EMDR is like a bulldozer to those roadblocks.

HOW EMDR CAN HELP YOU HEAL

As I mentioned earlier, nearly all your destructive patterns and negativity result directly from negative core beliefs that were developed during earlier life experiences, and which were not properly processed at the time. As a result, some aspects of those earlier life experiences (stimuli like: thoughts, bodily sensations, sights, sounds, smells, tastes, emotions, etc.) will likely remain stuck in your brain in unprocessed, raw form. Because of this unprocessed rawness, the brain becomes triggered to re-experience the raw data when it comes across something that reminds you of some aspect of that original experience. Basically, your brain becomes tricked into believing that the original experience is happening again—even though you may know logically that the experience happened well in the past (or at least is not happening now).

Let me give you an example to help illustrate this point. Imagine you are walking through the woods on a hike. While on this hike you come across a snake that bites you. Because the snake is venomous, you begin to hallucinate and feel sick. Your brain interprets that you are in danger, and your system begins to pump you full of adrenaline and all kinds of reflexive responses while you are in a total phase of fight-or-flight. (In this case, you begin to run as fast as you can towards the direction you consider as being safe.) You reach an office of some sort, and receive medical attention as you pass out, believing truly, that you are going to die.

Clearly, this situation above was traumatic, right? Now, suppose you've survived the snakebite. You have recovered physically and are back to your original health. Because the original situation happened so fast, you were so scared, and you entered a reflexive fight-or-flight mode, the original experiences would likely not be processed properly—they would remain in raw form. (Imagine the difference in the emotional "flavour" of the venomous snakebite versus what you had for breakfast this morning.) The aspects of the snake encounter will likely remain unprocessed—the shape of the snake, the colour, the sound it made as it slithered towards you, the hiss before the attack, the clothes you were wearing at the time, the terror you experienced as you ran, and the thoughts, "I am going to die."

Now imagine that you are visiting your best friend for a BBQ in their backyard. All your favourite people are there, and they are just waiting for you to join them and share your famous potato salad. As you arrive, you're so excited to see everyone and catch up; you are simply beaming with joy as you walk around the house to the backyard. As you begin to focus on your friends' faces, you catch the sight of a large snake coiled in the corner in the shade—you scream, drop the potato salad and run away to your car, lock the doors, and speed away.

What happened there? Your friend calls you to find out what they heck just happened, and after you begin to calm down now that you are sitting in the safety of your own living room, you explain to them that you saw a large snake and ran away—surely, they would have seen it too, right? Your friend takes a picture of their gardening hose, nicely wrapped up in the shade, and asks if this is what you saw. You logically conclude that, indeed, it could not have been a snake, but your chest begins to pound, and you still feel scared.

Because your brain has not processed the original snakebite incident, the raw data that comprised that experience remains stuck, and any current experience that shares a resemblance to you (i.e. the gardening hose resting coiled just out of the corner of your eye) will become information that triggers similar responses to that original experience (i.e. you become scared and want to run away).

EMDR works by assisting your brain to desensitize that original snakebite experience and reprocess the memory as something more accurate, and in most cases, positive.

Using our snakebite example, the belief that "I'm going to die" is obviously false (well, yes, we are all going to die, but probably not *right now*). The distress associated with that negative cognition ("I'm going to die") is eliminated, as is the associated stimuli (the sound as it slithered towards you, the colour of the snake, the pain in your leg, etc.). After the memory is no longer distressing, your brain would likely come to replace the negative cognition with a more positive one, such as, "I can protect myself," or "I'm OK now," or "I am strong." The feelings of fear would be replaced with feelings of calm, empowerment, or something that feels good.

If that's not cool enough for you, and what usually gets me, is when many of my clients will tell me that they've engaged in activities (that prior to EMDR treatment would have triggered an episode of distress), and they didn't even *realize* that they didn't experience any distress until after the activity is over. I often get a text or my client exclaiming to me at the start of our next session, "I didn't even have any anxiety! I didn't even think about my trauma!" It's incredible how EMDR heals people at such a deep level.

Pretty neat, eh? You may be thinking, "OK…so I get how the snakebite and the gardening hose connect, but I didn't go through a trauma like that. How can EMDR help *me*?"

Great question.

Let's say your complaint is somewhat vague, like, you want to feel more confident (a common one). Well, we would find out what your "inner critic" is really telling you about yourself (we all have an inner critic inside giving us the exact counter-argument to instil doubt in our abilities or experience). For example, if you're "not confident" maybe it means that you are "weak," or a "coward" (remember this is what your inner critic might be telling you, not what your logical more politically correct part of your mind might be telling you). So, let's say that the belief behind your lack of confidence is: "I am weak." Standard EMDR protocol would expand the aspects associated with this negative cognition, and then find the original roots of where this belief first came from, and eliminate the distress associated with that memory.

After the original root memory of the negative belief is reprocessed, you would be guided to find the example of when this belief and/or accompanying emotions and bodily sensations felt "the worst" in your life. After that is worked through, you would move onto more recent experiences, and work through those. Finally, the approach turns to the future where you and the EMDR therapist select one or more potential future scenarios where you would want to feel more confident in, and work through any doubt or fear associated with those situations. EMDR truly is a holistic approach, and one that I find very effective for many people.

After learning about what can be accomplished with EMDR treatment, or after an initial EMDR target has concluded, a typical response I get is, "Wow! This is amazing...but I don't understand, what is actually *happening* during EMDR?"

As you might remember, trauma causes the brain to store information as raw data in maladaptive ways—essentially the information is stuck on the right side of the brain (the more artistic, spatial, creative part of the brain). Because the left side of the brain has difficulty accessing the information on the right side, or it can only access tiny bits and pieces (i.e. as negative core beliefs), it's like the two sides of the brain are speaking different languages (my colleague's jazzy little analogy). EMDR helps each side of the brain begin to translate the information to the other and begin to speak the same language.

When you decide to seek out the aid of an EMDR therapist (in a later chapter, I'll help you with how to find the right therapist for you), you will inevitably undergo eight phases of treatment:

History

This phase of treatment is standard with all types of therapy. Here the therapist makes inquiries into your life and the history of the problem(s) you are seeking EMDR treatment for. Expect that a good therapist will ask you about early experiences in your life and your relationship with your parents and any siblings you have. This is called your <u>attachment history</u>. I ask my new clients a load of questions about what typical scenes are in my clients' early family life, what discipline looked like, if there were any complications during birth, if they moved residences often, any obvious signs of trauma (like physical or sexual abuse), if anyone died, if there's been any history with psychiatric illness in the family, etc.

Over the years I've become kind of a stickler with assessments, and I like all my new clients to fill out a host of them (probably because I like to work online with some people as well). So, expect that you will get some survey-type assessments to fill out. These assessments are not about passing or failing, but rather they are about getting a much clearer clinical picture of you prior to going deeper with specific memories.

Preparation

This phase of treatment is one that should occur throughout the course of treatment. In fact, I usually provide some element of this phase prior to getting a complete clinical history of my client—I like to know that my client has some tools to manage distress prior to potentially getting upset by thinking about the areas in their life likely to cause anxiety and discomfort. Think of it this way: It is better to learn how to apply the brakes prior to learning how to hit the gas.

Preparation is all about teaching you affect management techniques during session, and then witnessing you using those stabilizing techniques to bring emotional and/or physical distress down. Some of these affect management tools could be: The Container,

Calm Place, The Spiral, Light Stream, deep breathing, etc. All therapists trained by an accredited school (i.e. an EMDRIA-approved training course) will know these techniques. (If you already have a few techniques of your own that you use, and it works for you, your therapist will incorporate them into your treatment.)

For me, each session begins and ends with some combination of affect management. And sometimes it happens that as the individual gets deeper and deeper into the roots of their problem(s), newly emerging aspects of their psyche can initially feel a little destabilized. Thus having my client already quite aware of and practiced with using various stabilization techniques, allows my clients to have control over how to manage distressing feelings that might arise.

Assessment

During this phase you will be asked to think about a particular "target" (a target is a memory where the trauma really resides), and you will be guided to notice some very specific aspects of how that memory makes you feel. However, please note, that some in the EMDR community refer to EMDR as "Secret Therapy" because *it is not necessary for the EMDR therapist to know all the aspects of the traumatic memory*. This often takes a bit of the fear out of going into these memories for some people.

Desensitization

Here's where the "magic" really happens. By the very nature of thinking about something traumatic or upsetting, you will feel an increase in the amount of distress you are experiencing—it's just the name of the game. This cannot be avoided, unless you avoid getting any help at all for the problem, and simply live in denial. Don't worry though, the distress you might experience during EMDR treatment is worth it. If you think about the possibility of feeling that distress for just a little bit longer, and then you can finally "put it to rest" and no longer be plagued with those feelings, doesn't it seem like a decent trade-off?

I would have to say that all my new clients are amazed after the first memory they desensitize, because it no longer causes them to feel any distress. They say things to me like, "It's gone," "The memory feels really far away now," "It feels like a fact, there's no distress attached to it anymore," "The details of the experience don't seem sharp any more...it's sort of a blur now," etc. The desensitization of their first memory usually gives people a lot more confidence in this approach to therapy and provides a dose of hope for the next memory we work on!

Reprocessing

In the reprocessing phase of EMDR, you are encouraged to select (if you haven't already done so) a positive belief that you would *rather* like to believe about yourself in place of the memory you've just desensitized. You and the EMDR therapist work together to ensure that this belief *feels* completely true prior to moving on to the next phase. This phase of treatment usually feels quite positive.

Body Scan

Sometimes a tiny little bit of distress can remain lingering in the body. Here, the therapist invites you to scan your body from head to toe with your mind, and to detect if it feels like there's any tension or distress anywhere. If so, the therapist will help you to desensitize it.

Partial Future Template

I'm including this as part of the eight phases, but technically it's not explicitly listed in recent standard protocols, so imagine this as Phase 6.1. During this phase, you and the EMDR therapist will select a mini-scene that might occur in the future where you would need to deal with a similar kind of stressor (as your original stressor). Next, the EMDR therapist will ask you to imagine running the mini-scene from start to finish as you imagine coping effectively in the situation—while thinking of that positive cognition you just came up with. These aspects in combination together help to install the positive belief that you can face that potential future situation with confidence.

Should any distress arise while conducting the partial future template, it will also be desensitized prior to moving on. Sometimes, my clients still have a little bit of doubt in the back of their minds about engaging in a situation that previously caused them distress. That doubt should be worked through. When completed, it's always fun to check-in after they've successfully faced that future scenario. If there was any difficulty, it is simply more information to process during our next session.

Closure

This phase of treatment occurs in three distinct ways. The first and most frequent way the closure phase of EMDR treatment is experienced is after each session is completed. Any good EMDR therapist will ensure that you are properly grounded at the end of the session, assist you with containing any distressing aspects of the target (the memory you are working on), help manage expectations, and provide you with some instructions and guidance until your next session. Sometimes it is possible to completely work through a memory within one session, but it is by far the norm to need at least two sessions per memory (and, in cases of more complicated presentations of trauma, each memory can take considerably more time).

The second way that the closure phase of treatment occurs is when each target is completed. Your EMDR therapist will know that a target has been completed when all the distressing aspects of the target have been neutralized, the positive cognition is completely accepted, the body scan shows no tension, and the future scene has been run without problems. It is time then to move on to the next target. Your EMDR therapist should also mention that it's still possible that you could experience a slight return of distress prior to the next session. In my experience, this is usually not the case, but it can happen if the trauma had "many roots." Dr. Wilensky in my basic training course called this phenomenon "dust bunnies." I've taken to this affectionate term, and I normalize this possibility with my clients. Should they experience the presence of any "dust bunnies," a quick two or three-minute desensitization the next session is all that is usually needed to sweep them away for good.

The third (and my absolute favourite) way that the closure phase presents itself in EMDR treatment is with the conclusion of treatment. At this point, my clients have experienced a complete elimination of their symptoms and the reasons for entering treatment with me. On average, this occurs in about three or four months. There are cases where this takes quite a bit longer should there be an extensive trauma history to contend with. For individuals who have "simple" presentations of trauma (i.e. there really is only one incident of trauma), I have completed therapy within a handful of sessions.

Regardless of how long it takes to complete a target, the full issue, or treatment altogether, the next and final stage is something that is supremely important, and not to be overlooked.

Re-Evaluation

Proper EMDR protocols require that your therapist check-in with you about the previous or current target that you are working on. If the target has not been completed, then it is simply a check-in point that permits re-entry to the desensitization, reprocessing, or body scan phases, and usually sounds something like, "So, when you think of (the memory), what comes up for you now?"

When you have completed a target and you have moved on to the next target in the treatment sequence, your EMDR therapist should return to the previously completed target at the start of the next session, just to make sure there were no "dust bunnies" (tiny bits of lingering distress). When satisfied with the absence of distress, you and the therapist would simply move on to the next target and go from there.

Finally, the re-evaluation phase should, in some ways, be somewhat ongoing. After I have completed treatment with a client, I request a follow-up session at the one-month, three-months, and the one-year mark, just to ensure that no symptoms have returned. So far, I have not encountered a client whose symptoms have returned—this is because the results obtained with EMDR are forever-lasting. But, let's not be naïve, people are complicated, so I like to make sure the results have been sustained.

The follow-up sequence in my treatment also provides an opportunity for my clients to consider working on another issue if one is present. EMDR isn't an all-encompassing approach where eliminating one negative core belief means that you no longer have *any other* negative core beliefs. EMDR is great, but it's not a "silver bullet." For example, notice that the beliefs "I am worthless" and "I'm not good enough" are similar, so individuals *may* neutralize both; but the beliefs "I am worthless" and "I am a coward" are different. We can't assume that eliminating the belief "I am worthless" means that we don't need to also work on eliminating the belief "I am a coward." Now, of course, the *meaning* that one makes out of believing they are a "coward" might entail the feeling of being worthless underneath, so it may be possible to eliminate both, but I don't like to assume (you know what "ass u me" ing does, right?).

HOW TO GET THE MOST OUT OF EMDR

Signing up to begin EMDR therapy can mean different things to different people. Some will experience the undertaking as a sure sign that they are actively doing something to improve their lives, and, therefore, are excited! Others will experience the first few sessions in front of their therapist as a massive threat to their existing lifestyle. Change, to some of us, threatens the core of our feelings of safety (that is: Our routines keep us feeling safe—**stuck**—but safe).

I want to let you know about a few things when you're ready to undergo this process of personal evolution. First: *There is no way to fail at EMDR.* A good therapist practicing EMDR will take *all* information provided by the client as simply that: information. What the person says, doesn't say, how they visualize, or the troubles they have when attempting to visualize, etc., are all interactions that are considered as, "information." You needn't worry about "how well you're doing" when you're sitting in front of your therapist—that's for your therapist to evaluate (and let me be clear, the therapist is not judging you, they are looking for the best ways to assist you to move forward).

Secondly, *you must be truthful and honest with your therapist.* As much as some of us wish, we cannot read minds. I'm glad I can't—my imagination is already enough for me to contend with! Even if you do not wish to reveal some piece of information about your life or you have suppressed or cannot remember for whatever reason, do not lie to your therapist; this will greatly hamper your success in terms of time and can undermine the therapeutic relationship.

I find that it helps to simply say something like, "That's a part of my life I don't feel comfortable getting into right now."

Thirdly, to piggyback off that last point: *You and your therapist are both responsible for the therapeutic relationship.* It is a mutually agreed upon and co-facilitated relationship (although the therapist will undoubtedly shoulder more of the responsibility of directing the therapeutic process). The focus of the relationship is about 95% on you *always*, and only about 5% on the therapist. Traditionally, psychotherapy was thought to have had to be 100% focused on the client, but I find this to be an unrealistic expectation. If that were to be possible, the therapist would need to be completely inhuman—some form of artificial intelligence (such a possibility may not be that far off in the future, by the way).

As a human, the therapist will undoubtedly fall into self-reverie and contemplation of their own life in response to something the client is presenting. If determined to be beneficial, the psychotherapist will use this information to further the client's processing. Most therapists will agree with the notion that the therapist, him or herself, is one of their best instruments in any given session.

Back to the point about your responsibility for the therapeutic relationship: You are involved in interacting with another person. That other person has feelings (no matter how professional they are), and they can be hurt. As a human being, the therapist will make mistakes; when this happens, try your best to keep in mind that all humans are imperfect, and this can be an opportunity to in fact deepen, and strengthen the therapeutic relationship (if it is handled and discussed properly, of course).

The fourth note I wish to tell you about when you're undergoing the process of EMDR, is that *any therapist worth their wage, will not permit you to begin the desensitizing phase* before *you're properly prepared.* What this means with me is that every single therapeutic undertaking begins with some combination of taking patient history, providing stabilization techniques (teaching the client how to control—usually lower—their affective arousal [i.e. their distress]), and then preparing the client for the desensitization phase.

I usually describe to my new clients that I prefer to demonstrate how to "apply the brakes before we hit the gas" (I try to avoid this analogy with my motor vehicle accident clients, but every now and again the analogy just slips through). Like one of my EMDR supervisors said, "It's like imagining that you're driving down a steep, icy, mountainside with skinny, winding roads...you wouldn't want to hit the gas very hard, or you'd drive right off the cliff." We practice using the brakes and going slowly, so that when we're finally on a straight-away, we can floor it.

EMDR is amazing. There's no way around it. You can literally override your negative core beliefs and install new, more positive ones. But before you can get to the good stuff, you're going to have to go through the tough stuff.

Which brings me to the next point I want to make about how to get the *most* out of you EMDR therapy: *EXPECT distress*. The whole purpose of the treatment is to focus on the most distressing aspects of a trauma, so that you can finally get past it. Let me repeat that: You will be required to think about your distressing traumas one more time in your life so that you can finally put them away for good (well, you may still remember the memories, but they will no longer be distressing). You must know that you're ready for that. I often make the distinction to my clients that there's a *BIG* difference between feeling "safe" and feeling "comfortable." All my clients *must* feel safe with me, but I hope that most of my clients don't feel *comfortable*—otherwise we're not changing much. Like a colleague of mine once said, "Change happens on the edge of comfort."

How do you know that you're "ready"? If you can effectively utilize at least one or two affect management techniques, can think of your trauma and experience the corresponding negative feelings, emotions, core beliefs, and body sensations, and still feel present with the therapist, then you're ready—you are able to maintain dual attention. What do "feeling present" and "dual attention" mean? Let me explain.

"Feeling present" means that you can fully experience the moment at hand. You are mindful of your thoughts, the emotions your body maintains, as well as the therapist in front of you, and of the room you're in. You feel fully "here."

"Dual attention" means that you are "present" (as described above), *and* you can be aware of the distressing topic or trauma. This is actually very hard for some people whose traumatic memories force them to dissociate.

What's dissociation? You may remember we discussed this topic before, but here is another explanation that's important to consider when wanting to get the most out of EMDR therapy: Dissociation is a natural process that I believe occurs in most animals with more evolved brains. So I tend to think of dissociation as an evolutionary defense mechanism designed to respond to trauma.

As you may remember, any stressor that forces us to leave our "Window of Tolerance" (Ogden, et. al., 2006; Siegel, 1999); can cause us to dissociate—all in the interest of assuring our survival.

Dissociation occurs in the survival/reflex mode when the brain begins to operate differently from how it processes information under normal processing modes. The brain's focus is on survival, and thus begins to trigger the body to respond accordingly—it doesn't care about the accompanying stimuli it is still receiving. Our brains absorb millions of stimuli in any given moment, and it *still does* during extreme states of stress—it just stores it differently. So, when you experience similar stimuli to that original stressor, your brain will likely make you respond similarly—in a dissociative manner.

Dissociation is described in a somewhat unique way for everyone, you may remember that in my most extreme cases of dissociation,

I experience my consciousness "floating above my body," where I literally "see myself from the ceiling." Others experience dissociation as if their environment melts into them, and they "fuse" with others or the environment itself. Still, others have described their dissociative experience as if they are living as the star character in a movie or video game.

The more extreme forms of dissociation, will see individuals switch from personality to personality (as in Dissociative Identity Disorder—previously known as Multiple Personality Disorder), where they may or may not be aware of their switching. Although rare, Dissociative Identity Disorder is a method of dealing with extreme states of stress via dissociation (and it can be healed).

What's the whole point of this discussion about dissociation? For you to be prepared.

You may have to begin to master staying present before you can reap the rewards of EMDR therapy. If you are constantly dissociating, and not able to experience dual attention, then you are not ready for the desensitization phase of EMDR. Don't worry if you're not quite ready yet, you will be...in due time. Your therapist will help you.

My second-last point about how to get the most out of your EMDR therapy is to keep your therapist "in the loop" about what's going on for you. What you *don't* tell him or her can be just as important as what you *do* communicate. If something is happening for you between sessions and this is impeding on your life, it is probably important to cover in session. Allow your therapist the opportunity to help you to the full degree that he or she can.

Finally, do your homework on your therapist. Does your therapist belong to any established counselling or psychological memberships—preferably one or more that are concerned with championing a high standard of ethical practice? I belong to several myself: BC Association of Clinical Counsellors (governing the standard for how I conduct myself with my clients during and outside of my clinical sessions); EMDR Canada and EMDR International Association (concerned with upholding standards of EMDR practices and research); and the International Association of Counselling (concerned with providing access to ethically-sound counselling services across the world). Does the psychotherapist or psychologist belong to anything like these institutions? I would recommend that they do, otherwise they may not care about providing ethically-sound practice. By the way, "ethics" in this consideration is focused on the counsellor providing the client with services that are primarily concerned with ensuring the best safety measures, empirically-researched interventions and techniques; and any failure to do so will result in the counsellor being held accountable in some way.

You may also want to check where the counsellor or psychotherapist got their degree. Was it an accredited school? University? College? Or was it from Joe Blow's Internet College for Scam Artists? Depending on the country, state, or province where the counselling is taking place, various standards of ethical practice may also be required. Some countries have much more relaxed licensure requirements of their counsellors, so you may need to be diligent in your search.

When you're ready to begin searching for an EMDR therapist or practitioner, it's good practice to ask if they are a "Certified EMDR Therapist" or if they simply practice EMDR. There is a difference between a "therapist who practices EMDR" and a "Certified EMDR Therapist" (to become a Certified EMDR Therapist accredited by EMDRIA, the therapist must complete a certain number of supervision sessions with an accredited EMDR consultant, constantly be improving their skills by attending new trainings, and have conducted a large sample size of EMDR sessions with different clients). To be clear, even if the therapist is not yet a "Certified EMDR Therapist," I am not implying that they are not educated or not good at what they do; however, I personally would be hesitant to work with a therapist who isn't at least working towards their certification. To me, working towards becoming a Certified EMDR Therapist means that the therapist is very serious about how they conduct their sessions.

When you are ready to being your search for an EMDR therapist, there are two websites I recommend: EMDRIA's website provides a "Find a Therapist" search option that spans the entire globe (www. emdria.org), while EMDR Canada is concerned only with a searchable option for Canada (www.emdrcanada.org). Regardless, therapists who are listed on these sites are taking their EMDR practice more seriously.

When you have found a few EMDR therapists who seem intriguing to work with, don't be afraid to interview them. Therapy in general is a highly-individualized process, so just because one EMDR therapist might have loads of experience, they may not be the right fit for you. You will want to know some basic things about how they practice:

1. Make sure they explain to you how the initial phases of therapy are likely to progress. If their intake process is not lengthy, and you get the feeling that they are more concerned about how quickly they can get you in, I would be a little cautious. Seeing an EMDR therapist is indeed important but seeing the *right* EMDR therapist is even more important.

2. Notice what their history-taking (Phase One) is like. This for me goes hand-in-hand with my intake process as well as with my preparation/stabilization phase. If your EMDR therapist is not asking you quite a few questions about your childhood history, how you are currently functioning, what your current strategies to manage your stress are, and they haven't given you any types of assessments, then I fear that they are not going to get a full enough picture of you prior to desensitizing. There is a common phrase that EMDR therapists use to describe the early phases of treatment: Fail to plan, plan to fail.

3. Take into consideration whether you want to work in-person (the most traditional), or online (upcoming therapeutic frontier). Personally, I don't think anything can ever compare to working with a therapist one-on-one in the same room;

however, online video chat software has become a very close second. EMDR *can* be conducted online, and online counselling in general is becoming much more of a trend that appears to stay. I have conducted many EMDR sessions online with clients who have successfully transformed their lives. If you plan on going the online route, make sure your therapist has some specific safety plans in place for how they would work with you (online counselling, by nature, has a host of different concerns that in-person counselling does not).

4. Inquire about their cost for service. Treatment costs can range greatly. In British Columbia, Canada, the cost per average 60-minute session for a Registered Clinical Counsellor (RCC) is CAD $110.00. A psychologist in BC could run you upwards of CAD $200.00 per 60-minute session. I prefer to work in 90-minute sessions, but also utilize several different flexibility options depending on the needs of my clients—feel free to explore!

When you think about the total cost incurred when seeing a regular talk therapist versus an EMDR therapist, even if the cost per session is higher, the total cost for treatment with an EMDR therapist will undoubtedly be much lower overall. (For example: If you saw an averaged priced RCC weekly, for two years [a very common occurrence for someone in talk therapy], and they charged you CAD $110.00 per hour, you'd pay upwards of CAD $11,000.00. As I mentioned before, my average client spends about three months in EMDR treatment. That's quite the comparison.)

Some frequent questions, and concerns that I encounter from individuals at my live events, webinars, or during my free consultations are:

1. **Does EMDR hurt?**

   The simple answer to this question is, yes, and no. EMDR does not technically hurt, in the sense of physical pain (i.e. it's not like electro-convulsive therapy). However, since you are being asked to think about memories of yours that at the time when they occurred were likely to be very distressing, EMDR will elicit distress.

EMDR can be experienced as "extremely uncomfortable" for some, and for others, it might be experienced as only "mild to moderately distressing."

Since memories that have a physical or somatic element to it are likely to be "re-experienced" in session during the desensitization phase, I remind clients that this could be a possibility for them—and that it is a normal experience with EMDR.

The positive side of the "hurt coin" is that this period will likely be the last time that you experience that distress.

2. **What does EMDR *feel* like?**

EMDR feels like different things to different people. For some, desensitizing a target will be experienced as solely somatic; that is, they notice sensations in their body changing. For others, desensitizing a target will be highly cognitive, and perhaps only slightly somatic. For the majority, desensitizing a target will incorporate a little bit of "Column A" and a little bit of "Column B."

One of the most common responses I get after a lengthy desensitization session is that the individual feels like they've just had a workout. And that's exactly what's happening: The brain is working hard to rewire itself, so that's exercise—it might even burn calories!

3. **Are there any side effects?**

Yes. In some sense, EMDR does have some side effects. Because it's unlikely that a full memory will be completed in only one session, it means that the memory will be "opened" and then "closed" as "incomplete" by the end of one session. Therefore, it is rare that someone won't experience any kind of distress between sessions. What can be expected to occur while in the *process of working through a traumatic memory (or memories) is a return of **some** of the distressing symptoms associated with the memory. This happens because the traumatic material is being stimulated, and your brain is likely trying to "make sense of it."*

What might be experienced, could be: dreams, flashbacks, aspects of the traumatic memories being worked on, or entirely forgotten memories, memories that are "seemingly unconnected," and/or memories of sights, sounds, smells, etc.

On the positive side of things to expect between sessions is that the individual often begins to encounter scenarios in their daily life which are considered as being growth-oriented, adaptive, or "Mastery Experiences." These experiences assist individuals in attaining better and more accurate perceptions of themselves.

4. **Will it change who I am?**

Hopefully. The traumatic material that you are hanging on to has comprised an aspect of your identity. When that traumatic memory is no longer responsible for a negative core belief of yourself, you will begin to alter your perception of yourself. When this happens, you are changing.

When your identity begins to change, it is normal to experience symptoms commonly associated with grief (i.e. anger, fear, sadness, etc.). Even though it is likely that most of this change will come as a welcomed relief, don't be surprised if some part of you wants to resist that change.

5. **How quickly will I notice change?**

*This is a tricky question to answer because the speed of **noticeable** change for everyone will differ. I like to suggest that those who come with more complicated presentations of symptoms (such as: complex PTSD, personality disorders, bipolar disorder, etc.), and especially with those who are faced with tremendous amounts of chaos in their daily lives, will* *likely experience longer treatment times. This does not mean that mini-victories do not occur.*

Often these mini-victories signal the presence of deep change within the individual, and it is just a matter of time after desensitization has begun, when the individual will notice some more significant improvements.

6. **Do the effects ever fade?**

   No. The results of EMDR are forever-lasting. This is because the brain is adaptively "re-wiring" itself.

7. **How much detail do I need to go into with my therapist?**

   Not as much as with other therapies. EMDR is often called "Secret Therapy" because it is not necessary for the therapist to know every little detail about the traumatic memories that occurred to you. Generally, the therapist will want to know a little bit about the scene that is most disturbing to you, and then whether you are feeling "better," "worse," or "the same," or if what you experienced was "positive," "negative," or "neutral."

   An example of the point above is the following: Imagine the scene from earlier in the book where you were "bitten by a snake." The therapist does not need to know whether you were so scared that you urinated, or whether you dropped your camera, or whether you called for your mother. If the most disturbing part of the memory for you was seeing the snake leap at you, that is all you need to mention to the therapist. Sometimes, less is more. Now, with that said, if any of the above parts of the memory are particularly important to why you feel the memory is so disturbing and you feel that you need to share that, then by all means go ahead—most therapists have heard a lot and will not be shocked.

   It's possible that, at times, the therapist may inquire as to what you are experiencing if you or the therapist feel you are "stuck." This is a natural part of the process for many people and is simply a matter of allowing the therapist to "give you a little push." As always, feel free to share only what you feel safe enough doing.

8. **Can I do EMDR on my own?**

This is a tricky question. Some will say, "yes," and some will say, "no." There are self-help programs out there that are currently being studied to verify their safety for use with the public.

As a disciplined approach to trauma treatment, clinicians undergo extensive training to ensure the safety of their clients, and to perfect their adherence to EMDR protocols that are EMDRIA-approved. Trained trauma clinicians also have an awareness of trauma-related symptoms that are sometimes difficult for the "untrained eye" to notice, such as working with dissociative symptoms.

*Because EMDR treatment is highly subjective, one person's experience will not be the same as another's, therefore, it is difficult to state whether one person is likely to experi-ence a positive or a negative outcome with self-directed EMDR treatment. With that said, I have encouraged **some** individuals to incorporate bilateral eye movements, conduct tapping, or utilize audio tones on their own, between sessions when tackling chronic pain, addictions, or mild discomfort post-treatment.*

I recommend that, when deciding to utilize self-directed EMDR techniques, the individual consult with their EMDR therapist first.

9. **How long will treatment take?**

This is, again, rather subjective. Depending on the extent of one's trauma history, and how that trauma has become stored within the individual's neuro-networks, treatment time varies between everyone.

To some extent, the age of the individual can have a corre-sponding relationship with treatment time—that is, generally, the younger the client, the less likely they are to make a large amount of cross connections within neuro-networks. This tends to speed up the treatment times. However, individuals who have experienced extensive trauma at young ages can experience lengthy treatment times, even if they are still young.

After you and your EMDR therapist get a treatment plan together, your therapist should give you a pretty general idea as to how long treatment will take for your given situation.

A final note on this question is: While EMDR has extensive research to prove its effectiveness, new protocols are always being discovered and released. As the disciplined field of EMDR expands with new protocols, treatment times may as a result, become shortened.

10. **Is EMDR a form of hypnotherapy?**

This is a good question, and one that provided quite a bit of controversy during EMDR's early years after its conception. While EMDR looks somewhat like hypnotherapy, it is <u>NOT</u> hypnotherapy. The main difference between hypnotherapy and EMDR is that the EMDR therapist does not make any suggestions to their client, rather, it is the client's own internal system that does the healing—it is highly individualized.

11. **You've made it pretty clear that EMDR is your preferred form of psychotherapy; does that mean that you think that talk therapies like CBT or psychoanalysis are out-dated or useless?**

Great question. I really must be clear on this. I believe that all therapy is useful and has its place. Getting help is better than not getting help. Other forms of psychotherapy like CBT or Psychoanalysis, etc., can be a stepping-stone to more deeper work. Sometimes, talking it out is enough; the individual can process whatever their issue was and then live happily ever after. But sometimes that isn't enough.

I believe that, in the context of EMDR, talk therapy is useful in the sense that it helps the individual develop their skills in preparation for deeper trauma-based counselling.

That's about it, my friends. When you have found the therapist that you are excited to work with, try your best to "buy into" their counselling style. They do things the way they do because they've had experience to indicate that it works. Don't do anything that doesn't feel OK with you, and if you have questions or concerns with how they practice their EMDR, discuss them with your therapist. But "go all in" with EMDR. EMDR will work if you're willing to work with it (and your therapist).

If you have any questions about anything you've read, wish to book a FREE consultation, have any concerns, or if you want to offer me some feedback, I welcome all communication.

You can email me at: info@GrigoreCounselling.com. Please also feel free to check out and to "like" my Facebook page at: www.facebook.com/GrigoreCounselling. I'm also on Instagram as GrigoreCounselling, and my Twitter handle is @InfoGrigore. I look forward to hearing from you!

If you'd like to join my mailing list, you will gain access to some amazing and exclusive offers and be among the *first* to learn about upcoming live events and programs!

It has been an absolute pleasure to share with you. I truly wish you the best on your healing journey. And remember:

Life opens up when you do.

REFERENCES

Anxiety and Depression Association of America. (2010-2016). Understanding the facts of anxiety disorders and depression is the first step. Retrieved from https://adaa.org/understanding-anxiety

Aslani, J., Miratashi, M., & Aslani, L. (2013). Effectiveness of eye movement desensitization and reprocessing therapy on public speaking anxiety of university students. *Zahedan Journal of Research in Medical Sciences*, 46-49.

Beck, A.T., Ward, C. H., Mendelson, M., Mock, J., & Erbaugh, J. (1961). An inventory for measuring depression. Archives of General Psychiatry, 4, 561-571.

Bourne, E. J. (2010). The anxiety & phobia workbook (5th ed.). Oakland, CA: New Harbinger Publications, Inc.

Bryan, C. J., & Rudd, M. D. (2006). Advances in the assessment of suicide risk. *Journal of Clinical Psychology*, 62(2), 185-200. doi:10.1002/jclp.20222

Canadian Mental Health Association. (2017). Fast facts about mental illness. Retrieved from https://cmha.ca/media/fast-facts-about-mental-illness/

Croitoru, T. (2014). *The EMDR revolution: Change your life one memory at a time.* New York City, NY: Morgan James Publishing.

De Jongh, A., Broeke, E. T., & Renssen, M. R. (1999). Treatment of specific phobias with eye movement desensitization and reprocessing (EMDR): Protocol, empirical status, and conceptual issues. *Journal of Anxiety Disorders*, 13(1-2), 69-85.

EMDR International Association. (2017). EMDR International Association. Retrieved from http://emdria.site-ym.com/?

Gauhar, Y. W. M. (2016). The efficacy of EMDR in the treatment of depression. *Journal of EMDR Practice and Research*, 10(2), 59-69. doi:10.1891/1933-3196.10.2.59

Grant, M. (2015). Pain control with EMDR: Treatment manual (5th ed.). Australia: Mark Grant.

Grant, M. & Threlfo, C. (2002). EMDR in the treatment of chronic pain. *Journal of Clinical Psychology*, 58(12), 1505-20. doi: 10.1002/jclp.10101

Hazelden's Co-occurring Disorders Program. (2017). Screening and assessment for people with co-occurring disorders. Retrieved from http://www.bhevolution.org/public/screening_tools.page

Institute of Health Economics. (2010). The cost of mental health and substance abuse services in Canada: A report to the mental health commission of Canada. Retrieved from www.ihe.ca

McLeod, S. (2017). Maslow's hierarchy of needs. Retrieved from https://www.simplypsychology.org/maslow.html

Mental Health Commission of Canada. (2016). Making the case for investing in mental health in Canada. Retrieved from https://www.mentalhealthcommission.ca/sites/default/files/2016-06/Investing_in_Mental_Health_FINAL_Version_ENG.pdf

mindyourmind. (2013). Statistics Canada releases mental health survey results [Blog post]. Retrieved from https://mindyourmind.ca/expression/blog/statistics-canada-releases-mental-health-survey-results

Natha, F. & Daiches, A. (2014). The effectiveness of EMDR in reducing psychological distress in survivors of natural disasters: A review. *Journal of EMDR Practices and Research*, 8(3), 157-170. doi: 10.1891/1933-3196.8.3.157

National Institute of Mental Health. (2007). Always embarrassed: Social phobia (social anxiety disorder). *U.S. Department of Health and Human Services*, No. 07-4678.

Ogden, P., Minton, K., and Pain, C. (2006). Trauma and the body: A sensorimotor approach to psychotherapy. New York: Norton.

PopulationPyramid.net. (2010). Population Pyramids of the world from 1950 to 2100. Retrieved from https://www.populationpyramid.net/world/2010/

Protinsky, H., Sparks, J., & Flemke, K. (2001). Using eye movement desensitization and reprocessing to enhance treatment of couples. *Journal of Marital and Family Therapy*, 27(2), 157-164.

Siegel, D.J. (1999). The developing mind: How relationships and the brain interact to shape who we are. New York; Guilford Press.

The Mental Health Commission of Canada. (2016). Making the case for investing in mental health in Canada. Retrieved from https://www.mentalhealthcommission.ca/sites/default/files/2016-06/Investing_in_Mental_Health_FINAL_Version_ENG.pdf

Teeradej. (2017). Human brain model top view. Retrieved from www.stock.adobe.com.

Tidy, C. (2016). Panic attacks and panic disorder. Retrieved from https://patient.info/health/anxiety/panic-attack-and-panic-disorder

van der Kolk, B. (2000). Post-traumatic stress disorder and the nature of trauma. *Dialogues in Clinical Neuroscience*, 2(1), 7-22.

Van Ameringen, M., Mancini, C., Patterson, B., & Boyle, M. H. (2008). Post-Traumatic Stress Disorder in

Canada. *CNS Neuroscience & Therapeutics*, 171-181.
doi: 10.1111/j.1755-5949.2008.00049.x

Yalom, I. D. (1931, 1980). Existential psychotherapy. United
States of America: BasicBooks.

RESOURCES

Web links:

EMDR International Association Webpage: www.emdria.org

EMDR Canada Webpage: www.emdrcanada.org

The Francine Shapiro library: https://emdria.omeka.net

Grigore Counselling Website: www.GrigoreCounselling.com

www.ingramcontent.com/pod-product-compliance
Lightning Source LLC
Chambersburg PA
CBHW062347300326
41947CB00013B/1679